Marriage, Religion and Society

A HALSTED PRESS BOOK

Marriage, Religion and Society

Pattern of Change in an Indian Village

Giri Raj Gupta

JOHN WILEY & SONS

NEW YORK TORONTO

VIKAS PUBLISHING HOUSE PVT LTD
5 Daryaganj, Ansari Road, Delhi-110006
Savoy Chambers, 5 Wallace Street, Bombay-400001
10 First Main Road, Gandhi Nagar, Bangalore-560009
80 Canning Road, Kanpur-208001
17-19 High Street, Harlesden, London N.W. 10

Library of Congress Cataloging in Publication Data

Gupta, Giri Raj.
  Marriage, religion and society.

  "A Halsted Press book."
  Bibliography : p.
  1. Marriage—India. I. Title.
HQ670. G86   301.42'0954   73-5903
ISBN   0-470-33648-X

Published in the U.S.A., Canada and Latin America
by Halsted Press, a Division of John Wiley & Sons, Inc.,
New York

PRINTED IN INDIA

With his *Marriage, Religion and Society*, Dr Giri Raj Gupta joins the ranks of avid and articulate students of the sociology of village India. He has produced a village study with a difference: for the richness of its ethnographic content and for its insightful analyses, it will doubtless be classed among the better village studies done during the last two decades.

In this study of Awan, we get an excellent portrayal of the complexities of family, kinship, caste, and popular religion. The book will have, thus, a special appeal to students of marriage and the family. After describing the ecological and historical setting of the village, the author presents a brief but adequate account of the caste system as it functions in Awan. This was essential, for caste broadly defines the group within which marriages can take place. This is followed by an excellent account of the marriage rituals—their form and content. In this Dr Gupta has made a conscious effort to avoid tedious details, taking care at the same time to ensure that the essentials are not left out. The precision and restraint of his ethnography are commendable. He then takes up the social dimensions of marriage rituals for an extended discussion. The principal themes examined in this context are: intra-family roles and norms, implications of caste for marriage and the family, and social exchange among the castes. The *nata* alliance—remarriage—is considered in a separate chapter. In the scale of ritual purity remarriage does not rank high, but it is nevertheless practised among several of the lower caste groups. In the concluding chapter, major trends of change are discussed with a view to demonstrating how the traditional social system is responding to the challenges of modernisation.

Education, increased flow of communication, and economic development have contributed significantly towards changing the norms and values associated with marriage and family life.

Although the older generation bemoans the passing of tradition and the emergence of "crazy" ideas among the youth, it concedes that early marriages, though ideal for the traditional system, are becoming dysfunctional in the emerging order. It is also permitting an increasing degree of freedom in choosing mates, subject to the overriding consideration of caste endogamy. Ostentation and display, earlier a feature only of upper caste marriages, are being adopted by those sections of the lower castes who have acquired education and have improved their economic status. Rather than accept bride price, they now emulate the upper castes and offer substantial dowries.

The form and cultural context of marriage rituals have not undergone any major changes and continue to draw elements from the classical and the regional traditions. Some changes, however, are visible in this sphere; they emanate primarily from the unwillingness of some of the lower castes to offer menial services considered essential for marriage rituals. Occupational mobility is encouraging the growth of individualism, but kin-orientation built into the traditional pattern still asserts itself. It should be noted that secularised marriage law has had little impact on the community: marriage continues to be linked with religion, and caste councils continue to perform important regulatory functions. Changes are not uniform among upper and lower castes or among upper and lower income groups. This book has all this and a great deal more to suggest how, on the one hand, tradition is being modified and how, on the other, it is reinforcing itself.

Dr Giri Raj Gupta merits commendation on the excellence of this study. Some years ago I was impressed by the quality of his doctoral dissertation. In its present form, substantially revised for publication as a book, his thesis has acquired a sharper focus and greater clarity of expression. For this reason I am happy to introduce this book. As an example of analytical ethnography and as a contribution to the sociology of marriage and the family it will earn an enduring place for itself.

Indian Institute of Advanced Study,   S. C. DUBE
Simla

This book is a revised version of a dissertation submitted to the University of Rajasthan for the Ph.D. degree. The conclusions presented here were drawn from field research conducted in Awan village and its surrounding region in the Kota district of Rajasthan, India. Awan is the real name of the village and I agreed to use it because of the confidence the people placed in me and their insistence that it be used. Nevertheless, anonymity has been maintained regarding names of persons.

My first acquaintance with Awan dates back to June 1953. It was in the summer of 1956 that I had an opportunity to live for two months and visit several villages of Kota district under a College Youth Programme sponsored by the Ministry of Community Development, Government of India. My interest in village life was intensified by this sojourn, and for my Master's thesis in summer 1958 I selected Awan as the locus of my future research. I embarked upon the study of ritual aspects and their relation to the social structure of the community. Soon I was convinced that I needed to confine my inquiry to only a few aspects to produce a well rounded and intensive study, and I decided to concentrate on the interplay of marriage, religion and social structure. However, it is not my intent to claim that such an objective has been fully met in this book.

Field trips in 1963-65 were financed by a travel grant from the University Grants Commission, New Delhi, while I was teaching at the University of Udaipur. I accepted a teaching position at Western Illinois University in the autumn of 1969, where increased time and facilities for the revision of the manuscript were made available to me. The Research Council of Western Illinois University generously funded secretarial and research assistance for the revision of the manuscript. To all these I express my grateful appreciation. However, the responsibility for the analyses stated in the book rests with me alone.

I am especially grateful to the people of Awan, their kinsmen and friends, who unhesitatingly gave me information, and without whose cooperation this book could not have been written.

I owe a special debt of gratitude to Professor Brij Raj Chauhan for his guidance, unfailingly humane interest and creative teaching; to Professor McKim Marriott for his invaluable advice, criticisms as well as many kindnesses; to Professor S. C. Dube for inspiration, generous encouragement and especially for writing the Foreword to this book.

In various phases of field-work and writing I have benefited from the contributions of many people, among whom I should like to mention discussions with Professor Adrian C. Mayer and the contributions of Professors M. N. Srinivas, David G. Mandelbaum, Milton Singer and Harold A. Gould.

I also want to thank Professor John R. C. Morton, Assistant Dean of Graduate School and Research, and my colleagues Professor Grant Bogue and Dr Igolima T. D. Amachree at Western Illinois University for their continued interest in my research.

Thanks are also due to Tim Newport for his editorial assistance, and to Deborah McConnell and Allene Simpson for skilful secretarial assistance.

My wife has helped me in interpreting the marriage rituals discussed in the original Sanskrit *Dharmasastras*, in preparing the index and glossary and organising the material for the press.

For permission to reproduce in somewhat revised form some portions of this book, the author is thankful to the following publications in which the material first appeared: *Udaipur University Research Studies* for "Social Mechanisms and Institution of Remarriage in a Rajasthan Village," 3 (1965: 24-36), and to the *International Journal of Sociology of the Family* for "Religiosity, Economy and Patterns of Hindu Marriage in India," 2 (1972: 43-53).

August 1973   GIRI RAJ GUPTA
Macomb, Illinois

Contents

The traditional Hindu marriage has far greater significance than the simple unification of man and woman in the matrimonial state. Through the Hindu marriage an insight can be gained into the complex network of kinship ties, the entanglement of religion with the social structure, the functioning of the caste, the relationship between castes, and the cohesiveness of the extended family unit. Marriages reinforce and refurbish the socio-religious structure which has existed in India for centuries. For this reason the object of this study will be to describe and analyse marriage, religion and the social structure of Awan—a medium-sized Indian village community. Awan is located in south-eastern Rajasthan. According to Karve's classification of kinship zones in India, the village lies in the central zone, leaning more towards the northern zone (Karve 1965: 164). Although the focus of this study is a village, the network of marital ties encompasses a wider area of kinship than that of the village itself.

The study uses the terms "marriage", "religion" and "social structure" and their interrelationships within the context of the village community of Awan and its kinship region. These concepts have been clarified by earlier works in ways well suited for presentation or analysis of the field material from a variety of village communities. After taking brief note of the formations of these concepts, it is necessary that their relevance to the data from Awan be stated.

In relating several aspects of marriage to the general ethico-religious and structural values, it seems important that we look into the social implications of the rituals of marriage thoroughly, A brief discussion on the uses of certain basic terms seems to be imperative at this stage.

Marriage has been defined by Westermarck as "a relation

of one or more men to one or more women which is recognised by custom or law and involves certain rights and duties, both in the case of the parties entering the union and in the case of the children born of it" (1925:26-27). The definition is a comprehensive one which covers almost all marriages. The definition identifies cases of one man marrying one or more women, calls attention to the existence of recognition by custom, and recognises that the rights and duties of the mates and children are central to the union. This definition allows the data for Awan to be analysed in a universal sense. It would, however, be profitable to note how marriage customs operate at the village level in Awan.

Two forms of marriage, the *byav* (colloquial use of the Sanskrit word *vivah*) and *nata* exist in the village. The first type of marriage in which a maiden is married to a bachelor, divorcee or a widower is called *byav*, *vivah* or *shadi*. This must be the girl's first marriage. Her status is *kanya* and only in this state is the ceremony of *kanyadan*—the gift of the girl to a suitable mate—performed. Higher sacred values are placed upon this kind of marriage, which in turn brings greater prestige to the parents of the bride and the groom. Marriages such as these involve heavy expenditure, elaborate ceremonies and public performance of the roles in the presence of members of the kin group, caste and the village community. These costs have a direct bearing on the prestige allocations of the members within the caste and affect patterns of selection and the chances for marriage.

Among the twice-born castes, i.e., the Brahmin, Rajput and Mahajan, a girl could be married only once in her lifetime. Marriage is considered to be irrevocable and indissoluble. Among the non-twice-born castes a girl is allowed to remarry. However, no girl once married can go through the full wedding rites a second time. A girl's second marriage, performed without full wedding rites, is known as *nata*. It is uncommon to see an upper caste widow remarrying or an upper caste girl deserting her husband to remarry. By making use of this custom the women of the non-twice-born castes desert their husbands, seek divorce and often remarry after the death of their husbands. Thus *nata* entails a simple ceremony and is a less expensive form of remarriage.

While *nata* marriages are considered legitimate the ritual

and social status of a girl married through full ceremonies is higher. In polygenous families the first wife, who is usually married through full wedding rites, has a superior status to that of others. However, the man usually looks after the new wife with greater care. The children in either case are considered legitimate and the rights of inheritance and succession follow accordingly. Theoretically, intercaste marriages are prohibited. When upper caste men are found to have mistresses from castes other than their own, social recognition is not generally extended to such unions. Children from such unions belong to the mother's caste and inherit nothing from the father.

The term "ritual" has been extensively used in the work. Since rituals represent basic premises of religion and form the core of organised religion, the association of ritual with religion stems from the distinction made between magic and religion by Frazer, who suggested that chronologically magic preceded religion (1956:63-64). Durkheim regarded magic as essentially individual and anti-social, although he thinks that the magical rites are, in many respects, similar to religious ones (1961:58). Marett advances the argument that magic does not form a part of an organised cult and tends to be regarded by the society concerned as illicit (1915:146). Such an exclusion of magic from ritual and insistence of the idea that ritual relates only to religion hampers research into the nature of rituals. In villages like Awan, the rituals recorded in a marriage ceremony contain magical elements and cannot be explained without recourse to the inclusion of magic. In this connection, Radcliffe-Brown's view of studying ritual without getting involved in the theoretical dichotomy of magic and religion, sacred and profane, provides a helpful starting point (1965: 114-122). Nadel clarified the point by combining religious and other repetitive rituals having no connection with the mystical or the supernatural in the study of ritual and suggests "any type of behaviour may, thus, be said to turn into a ritual when it is stylized or formalized and made repetitive in that form" (1957:99). It is in this last sense that the term "ritual" shall be used in this inquiry.

Another aspect of our discussion in this treatise has been the relationship of marriage and religion. It has been our purpose to diagnostically present the specific functions of religion associated with different duties, rites and performers, to demonstrate that the ritual complex of Hindu marriage is geared to norm-setting, status affirmation and cooperation-ensuring functions.

Religion as used here means a system of beliefs and acts performed by the members of a society expressed in its values placed upon the concept of the supernatural. Viewed in this way, the term "religion" will include symbols, myths and rituals described in pure cosmology as well as pragmatic "magical" devices used to cure, exorcise or propitiate certain superhuman or supernatural powers (Mandelbaum 1966:1174). Although the formal outlines of Hinduism are fairly well known since they are clear and simple, it is at the empirical level that its content becomes highly incomprehensible and infinitely complex. At the operational level Hinduism practised in daily life, rite of passage, and the annual cycle of fasts and festivities are not quite the same as the Hinduism of the classical sacred texts. Variations exist in the applications of norms to the different levels of the social hierarchy which make the analysis difficult.

The term "structure" implies "the ordered arrangement of parts" in such a manner that "while parts themselves are variable" their arrangement has a relatively constant position (Nadel 1957:8). In applying this term to social fields, Nadel notes the differences in the choice of units made by various writers. Empirical studies are facilitated as one starts with the simplest of the units. Radcliffe-Brown maintains "the components of social structure are human beings", the structure itself being an "arrangement of persons in relationships institutionally defined and regulated" (1950:82). His position, that human beings are not to be considered as organisms but as occupants of positions in the social structure is well known (1952:9-10). This point has received further corroboration in Parson's insistence on the study of social relationships "between actors in their capacity of playing roles in relation to one another" (1949:34). Nadel has further explicated the theme in his *Theory of Social Structure*. Evans-Pritchard has stressed the need for including only interrelationships of groups and excluding interpersonal relationships from the scope of social structure (1946:262). In the present work this line of approach has not been feasible. Marriage implies a relationship between two sets of kin groups; however, on a number of occasions decisive roles are played by individuals who hold defined positions in relation to the bride and bridegroom. The prescribed norms of such relationships and the actual behaviour of persons so placed enable one to identify the positions of the participants correctly. In this study the term "social structure" will include pattern and network of social relations among individuals occupying defined social positions and cover both the norms and the behaviour of the people vis-a-vis these norms. Apart from the individuals so placed, the position of caste, clan and lineage will be examined for the major social groups of the village.

Among the writers who have laid sound foundations for the study of rituals in relation to social structure, two stand out significantly: van Gannep and Emile Durkheim. As early as 1909 van Gannep (1960) examined the significance of rituals from the social point of view, classifying them into three categories: rites of separation, transition and incorporation. He saw "regeneration" as a fundamental law of life and the universe: the energy which is found in any system gradually gets depleted and needs renewal at intervals. This is accomplished in the social world by the *rites of passage*. Gannep's classification of the rituals of marriage into separation, transition and incorporation elucidates the state of the individual through the *rites of passage* or the major events of life, but entirely lacks an explanation of how the norms work through these social states. In examining the data from the present study, one can see that marriage does not separate the individual completely from the group, but incorporates him in addition into another group. The rites of transition are practised throughout the life span of the individual, and thereby fail to provide a lucid view of the permanent status of the individual. The classification of rites requires some refinement for embracing cases where incorporation in one group does not amount to separation from the earlier group and where an individual continues to hold a status allocated to him.

The second major theoretical contribution has been Durkheim's work, *The Elementary Forms of the Religious Life*. The importance of rituals as accounted for by their social function is classified into four categories: the disciplinary and preparatory function, the cohesive function, the revitalising function and the euphoric function (Durkheim 1961:337-461). While this classification explains the functions of rituals for society as a whole, it avoids explanation of the category of a ritual by which the status of the individual is recognised. The cohesive, revitalising and euphoric functions can conveniently be merged into one category since they are utilised as a means for ensuring the cooperation of the groups and saving them from disintegration and depletion. The difficulties faced in the classificatory schemes noted so far for encompassing the nature of rituals and their relationship in the social structure of the village community of Awan can be resolved by following a threefold classification of rituals according to their relevance to the social structure: (*i*) norm-setting aspect of the rituals; (*ii*) status-affirmation aspect of the rituals; and (*iii*) cooperation-ensuring aspect of the rituals.

The present study thus involves an understanding of the village community and its heterogeneity. This work has been attended to in Chapter II. The social structure of the community involves an identification of the units—the castes and their internal organisations to which Chapters III and IV have been devoted. The details of the rituals from the stage of anticipatory socialisation to wedded life have been described in Chapters V, VI and VII. Marriage involves the active playing of roles of persons in their capacities as members of the family, kinsmen, and members of the caste in several defined positions. The norms and practices relating to these have been studied in Chapters VIII, IX and X. The institution of marriage differs significantly in its form and pattern among the various caste groups. First and subsequent marriages involve differential observance of rituals. And again, through emphasising the elaborateness of rituals, and their close association (imitation) with the practices of the higher castes, the castes of the middle range hope to raise their status. Some effects of this desire are beginning to be discerned in the type of participation of members of different caste groups in marriage ceremonies. The Chapter on social exchange among castes is especially designed to the actions taken to achieve this objective. Conclusions of the study are essentially limited to the area and the period of inquiry.

The field work for the present study was undertaken between 1958 and 1965. The data relate to 321 marriages occurring from 1936 onwards, and to 170 remarriages from 1936 to 1965. However, only 67 marriages and 11 remarriages were celebrated during the period of field work in the village and its vicinage which were personally observed and investigated at different stages of ritual observance. The information was collected through interviews with persons recalling their own marriages as well as those occurring in their own families. The work incorporates the data for the period indicated above for 19 castes and notes the differential picture of ritual elaboration in marriages, patterns of mate selection, the age at marriage, education, economic aspects of marriage, the functions of caste and subcaste councils and intercaste relations.

In sum, this exposition is intended to present an analysis of the complexities of centuries-old social structure of an Indian village which is facing the early challenges of modernisation. By presenting a microcosmic picture of the village social environs from inside, the complexities of family, kinship, caste, religion, and their intricate relationship with the vast system of Indian society, it is assumed that the reader will see it as a dynamic whole, a part of an interdependent system with extensive possibilities of innovation and change.

Awan, the focus of this study, a village of 2,574 people distributed among 41 Hindu castes and 6 Muslim caste-like groups, is located in Kota district of south-eastern Rajasthan, India. The region which embraces the three contiguous districts of Kota, Bundi and Jhalawar is named Harauti. "Harauti" is a term derived from "Hara", a clan among the Rajputs which founded a princely kingdom in the thirteenth century at Bundi from which Kota and Jhalawar emerged as other princely states in 1631 and 1838 respectively (Das, Shyamal 1888d: 1407, 1483).

THE ECOLOGICAL SETTING

Geographically Harauti lies in the sub-region where the Aravalli ranges touch Malwa. The matrix of the ranges and the dense forests is known as "Darah", which is about eight miles from the village. Awan is among those villages which have a location on a rich soil area. The Chambal river divides the region, and the village under study lies in the eastern half. Awan has communication links with the sacred land *Brij Bhumi* on the northern and Malwa on the eastern side. The village is situated at 25° north of the equator and 76.1° east of Greenwich. The region is a plateau with a mean elevation of 1,800 feet or 555 metres above mean sea level and is about 400 miles from the nearest sea coast. The topography of the area is uneven, with some hillocks rising to 3,000 feet. The area forms a vast tableland with richly fertile fields, wells, ponds, brooks and seasonal rivers. The Chambal, Kali-Sindh and Ahu are the important rivers of the surrounding region.

The climate of south-eastern Rajasthan is very different from the other parts of Rajasthan. This region is covered

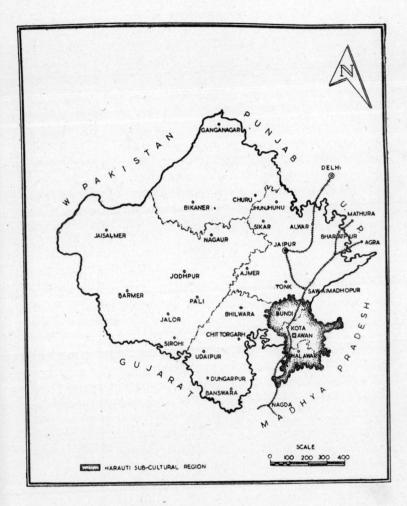

Fig. 1. Map of Rajasthan showing Harauti sub-cultural region.

with dense forests and stretches of green fields. The climate is variably moderate and while the temperature goes beyond 100° F daily in April, May and June, it generally cools at night. The rainy season extends from the middle of June to the middle of September, resulting in an average annual rainfall of forty inches. Rainfall, however, is so variable that it occasionally spoils crops and adversely affects the economy. The winter begins in October and becomes milder by the month of January. The weather is usually dry and comparatively warm with an average temperature of 80° F. Evenings and nights are cool enough to require warm coverings. The rainy season turns the village's yards and streets into a sea of mud. Only a patch of the market which is paved with stones remains dry. The transitions between the seasons of summer, rain and winter are pleasant. The monsoon from the south-east of the country, rising from the Arabian Sea, is the main source of showers in the rainy season, but the winter also has some showers from the local and retracting monsoon.

Because of its location on a hill, all the water resources lie outside the village. The water level varies from an easy approach to 50 feet. A shallow pond is used by the villagers for washing and bathing. When the pond dries during the summer, bricks are made from the clay at the bottom. For irrigation, more than a hundred wells are located over the patches of cultivable fields. Some of them occasionally serve for drinking water as well.

To the visitor, the village presents a picture of houses situated on an elevated mound of debris 25 to 100 feet from the general level of the surrounding plain. The village contains many wells, gardens and shrines of deities. *Imli* (tamarind), *aam* (mango), *neem* (margosa), and *pipal* (fig) trees and small thorny shrubs which fence the fields grow abundantly. The black soil around the village is well suited to growing wheat, gram, linseed, peas, and pulses, while the adjacent patches of uncultivated land provide grazing land for the herds of cattle. The area and distribution of the fields is uneven. Small channels supply water scooped from wells with *charas* (large leather or iron buckets) drawn by a pair of oxen. During the crop season the fields are adorned with various shades of green. The village has a reputation for raising agricultural crops well above the average of the surrounding region.   After the crop has been harvested, the villagers' work becomes husking grains and transporting them either to *bandas* (store-rooms), *khais* (deep cellars) or markets. From the fields the centre of activity shifts to the village market where brisk transactions of crop products and straw take place. Rope making, thatching, brick making and house repairs replace the work on the fields.

THE VILLAGE AND ITS CULTURAL AND LINGUISTIC REGION

People in Rajasthan speak a number of dialects which are collectively known as Rajasthani.   Harauti and Khariboli, the two major dialects, are the mother tongue of 46 per cent and 39 per cent of the population respectively.   All but 2 per cent of the remaining 15 per cent claim either Urdu, Malvi, Braj Bhasa, Marwari, or Sindhi as their mother tongue (*Census of India* 1961: 226-237).   Most of the inhabitants of Awan speak Harauti, although some of the migrants such as Sikhs and Khatris use Panjabi in their homes.   All the Muslim groups speak Harauti and occasionally Khariboli and Urdu.   The impact of Braj Bhasa and Malvi on the area may be observed in accents and modulations of syllables in the pronunciation of certain words.   The people's use of Khariboli in the region illustrates the impact of the Braj Bhasa form of Hindi.   From the Moghul times, the influence of Delhi in political as well as cultural matters placed the region within the orbit of Hindustani or Hindi (Chatterji, S. K. and S. M. Katre 1965: 401).

Mythical Connections
The village provides a complex variety of explanations of its evolution into its present social structure through a history imbued in secular and sacred legends.   Some of the relics of the historical past provide clues to the probable origin of the village.   Mukandara, the bifurcating range of the Aravalli mountains, is considered to be a historical wall which has always guarded the village of Awan from invasions since feudal times.   The mythical name of Awan was Kolia Patanpur which people sometimes refer to as the original name of the village.   The ancient relics of the *Popan ka Ravala* and *Popan Pol* receive their names from Popan, a female ruler of Awan known for her

maladministration.[1]

Archaic monuments in the form of small shrines of "Khodian" and "Sarnia" as the abode of Siva, and an old temple of Badri-narain (one of the incarnations of Lord Vishnu), although comparatively recently developed, and the shrine of Maha Kaleshwar and Bhata-devta attract notice. The temple of Lord Badrinarain was probably established in the fourteenth century in the area covered with dense forests which provided a place for saints and devotees. Now 98 per cent of the village population belongs to the sect which follows him.

Written documents regarding the factual existence of Popan are not available. But the architectural monuments, referred to as the palaces of Popan, live in the memory and recollection of the people. The archaeological pieces in stone indicate that Popan's time might have been quite prosperous and provided sufficient incentive to the development of art and culture. The name of this female ruler has been transferred to some of the architectural monuments, four of which, located on the four corners, are significant. These four, made completely of stone and therefore still surviving, are said to be the shrines of Mahadeva, the Lord Siva, whose emblematic images are found in the inset quadrangle of the temples. These four temples are situated at the four corners of the village, but two of these temples also have images of Jain deities, most probably of Lord Mahavira, in the central place and in the carved motifs of the stone. This corresponds to the architectural design of the fifth and sixth centuries. The other two shrines of Mahadeva are comparable to the great temples of the south in their form and engravings. It is probable that these two cultures flourished greatly in their own times. The *Torandwar*, or the diadem gates, which are now in ruins, further attest to the existence in these parts of the achievements of civilisation. The deserted palaces of Popan, now reconstructed and modernised, house the recently established Higher Secondary School.

It is said that Popan was a devotee of Lord Siva and she ordered

[1]It is quite probable that Popan actually lived since the myth is popular not only in Rajasthan but Gujarat also. Some folklorists have different views, claim that Popan was a wife of a potter, well known for foolishness, who lived in Khandela, a part of Jaipur State, or that she was born in the ruling families of Gujarat and was well known for her benevolence (Sahal, K. L. 1958 : 109).

all her people to worship Him. Her mother-in-law used to accompany her during the worship. Another ruler, Arnoraja, the grandson of Prithviraj I, had a play written which showed to his people his devotion to Siva. The *Harakeli*, written between 1160 and 1170, depicts Arnoraja defeating enemies with Siva's blessings.

The four shrines are known as Popan and the school area as the ruined palaces of Popan. Some 200 places, such as trees, wells, other water spots and some of the fields have the plank-like shrine of Siva with his gravelled stone emblem in the centre, marking the impact of Siva on the religious life of the people. Devotees keep the *pradosh* fast either on Mondays or on days specially assigned through astrological calculations, which occur once in a fortnight.

THE HISTORICAL PERSPECTIVE

The historical monuments displaying the figures of Buddha engraved in the rock panels suggest that this area was once populated by followers of Buddhism. This period would date back to the time when the Chauhan branch of Rajputs had not entered this region. The motifs also indicate that probably Jainism had also found its way among the people. The archaeological remains surrounding the village compel one to conclude that the buildings now ruined may have been the centres of learning and devotion.

Due to the influence of the Jain *acharyas* of the time (*circa* 1106 A. D.), Jainism had either the favour or the active and steady support of a number of Chauhan rulers. Prithviraj I obviously looked favourably on Jainism when he had a golden cupola put on the Jain temple at Ranthambore in 1078 A. D. (Sharma, M. L. 1938: 53) and his son Ajayaraj presented a golden *kalasa* to the Parsvanatha temple at Ajmer (Sharma, D. 1959: 227). His descendants even prohibited throughout the dominion the slaughter of animals on Jain holy days and donated the revenue of some of the villages to the Jain temples.

On the other hand, Prithviraj I was a follower of Saivism, as the Chauhan *prasasti* refers to Someshvara, meaning Somnath and Ajayaraj. His son was also a devotee of Siva, but he is known to have also paid due respect to the followers of Vaisnava and Jain sects (Sharma, D. 1959 : 38-40). This indicates that before 1143 A. D. and in the following decades different religious sects under the banner of Hinduism were flourishing under royal patronage. The only marked characteristic of their unity was their professed belief in the Veda, a belief which allowed them the widest latitude of thought and action. This belief may have resulted in heterodoxical systems of belief.

Vaishnavism, as a school of thought, has found occasional favour among the rulers. For example, Prithviraj II and Prithviraj III took pride in being regarded as incarnations of Rama. But Saivism found the greatest acceptance throughout the Chauhan dominions. The region is credited with the construction of many Saiva temples and shrines and establishing many places for devotees to engage in religious discussions and preaching. The region of Harauti seems to have received its name from Lord Siva. Harauti is a combination of "*Hara*", meaning Siva, and "*auti*", meaning *oat* (a Sanskrit word meaning protected), i.e., Siva's protected region. This is a region where the tenets of Siva have permeated the lives of the people. Siva is represented most often in the form of the *lingam* or *linga*, which are so frequently found and lavishly adorned that one would find in almost every temple a reference to names such as Siva, Mahadev, Shanker, Hara, and Trilokinath. At certain spots the *Mukhilinga* form of Siva is found, its upper cupola form being indicative of *Brahmanda* (the universe), the eastern side bearing the figure of the sun, the northern that of Brahma, the western of Vishnu and the southern of Rudra. Thus, the whole image is not only of Siva but also the other highly philosophic conceptions of Rudra, Surya, Vishnu and Brahma—the other manifestations of Lord Siva. Many princely rulers in Rajasthan paid homage to the Lord Siva who was considered the master of the land and the state. The ruler was merely his representative (Das, Shyamal 1888a:317). One of the oldest abodes of Siva in Awan is said to be the *math* of Lord Siva where one *sadhu* of the Babaji caste was buried alive in a trench. The shrine of Siva was established on his tomb by the heirs of the Babaji, probably in the eleventh century, when the village did not have a large habitation.

During 1300, Samar Singh, son of a feudal ruler, Dev Singh, began his reign at Bundi. The Bhils who lived in the surrounding areas invaded many parts of the state and looted the area. Samar

Singh drove them back to the other regions. A battle for peace and tranquillity was fought near Akelgarh village in which the leader Kota was killed. The spot and its surrounding region was named Kota after him (Sharma, M. L. 1938: 61; Mehta, M. N. and M. N. Mehta, 1896: 334). The Brahmin, Rajput, Mahajan, Mali, Kachhi, Dhakar and Sunar have their *sati* monuments in the surrounding area of the village and the members of the caste worship them on occasions, particuarly on the day of *Ashtami* which occurs twice a year. The crimson colour on some of the slabs affirms that people worship these *satis* in the form of their lineage and caste deities. The custom of *sati* was principally practised in feudal times. When a man was killed in battle his wife was either cremated alive with his corpse or ceremonially immolated herself later as a mark of fidelity to her brave husband. In memory of such persons slabs have been erected.

The above discussion of the region of Harauti illustrates the difficulty of pinpointing a date when the village first appeared. Research into the history of the region and its rulers has shown that the village has a confused picture of its past with no clear vision of where the truth lies. Historical facts reveal a clear consistency only at the later stages. The people of the village are neither able to give a clear description of their ancestors nor is Awan's leadership accurately traced by early records. Awan, the princely capital of Kota to which it has belonged since 1631, has existed since the early Christian era and thus has experienced many varied cultures.

Though we must be wary of the exaggerations the people tend to make to support the antiquity of their village, caste and progenitors, we need not ignore certain obvious facts. The hill of debris on which the village is located has many layers of houses and temples. The old polished walls and the engraved rocky structures under the surface validate the fact that the village has undergone many changes.

Some stray instances from historical documents show that the village existed during the reign of the great Akbar. Awan-Bosamir was a part of Ranthambore division and comprised 25,747 *bighas* of land in 1590 (Fazl-I-Allami 1949: 280). The latter appendage either has been lost in the course of time or was a complementary name of some other village.

Another event recorded in history which helps date the village was a struggle for power between two claimants to the heirship of the Kota state in 1638. During the reigns of Alamgir, Visnu Singh and Ram Singh, the sons of Kishan Singh, the late ruler, became involved in the conflict and that led to a battle at the village of Awan (Das, Shyamal 1888d: 1412)

Since the inception of the Kota state on 1 December 1631, which included *paraganas* of Kota and Palayatha under the hereditary Jagir of Madhu Singh, second son of Rao Ratan of Bundi, the heirship of the Chauhan Rajputs of the Hada tribe continued till the British rule in India (Mehta M.N. and Mehta M.N. 1896: 334; Singh R. 1951: 101-2).

Awan has a long history and the archaeological monuments indicate reasonable prosperity. Recent memories of the people include the visit of His Highness Maharao Bahadur of Kota, who used to visit the village on state tours. A camp would be established at the outskirts of the village to welcome him since his visits were events of importance. They occasioned the review and sanction of provisions for the villagers. The village elite, government officials, and the important people of the castes expressed their views on certain matters to him. People of older generations remember the heyday of their time when kind consideration was shown to the villagers by the Maharao Bahadur in constructing the village tank and *kharanja* (paving) on the main street of the village. Before 1947 Awan had a primary school and the office of the *patwari*.

Awan has two major religious groups: the Hindu and the Muslim. The first comprises 41 caste groups and the latter is divided into 6 caste-like groups. Members of these groups have traditionally been allotted certain functions. The groups have been arranged in a hierarchical order in practices relating to acceptance of food and water. Every caste group has a distinctive social life and set of ritualistic practices. The idea of purity and pollution has a specific meaning for every caste, but for reciprocal relations castes are regarded as pure and impure, clean and unclean. Certain castes are considered to be untouchable. The concept of ritual purity varies from one caste to another, though there are certain castes which may be grouped together from this point of view. All the castes have their own ritual configurations by which the ritual status is determined. Where more than one caste stand at the same or nearly the same level of ritual hierarchy, the same stratum groups them. A similar caste often unites with other groups of a similar nature and status when they share a common goal.

The caste has two types of organisations from the spatial point of view. The first is limited to the village itself and the other spreads over a number of villages in the region.

Pattern of Dwellings

The village of Awan overlooks surrounding fields and nearby villages. The village does not seem to have been constructed according to a definite plan. Two main streets, approximately a furlong each, cross at the main market. These have become the main lanes of the village. The boundary of Awan is demarcated by the mound itself on which it is located. The bus-stand, the ponds and the village well are located on the western boundary which is lined by the bus route running between the Tehsil Headquarter Sangod and District Headquarter Kota. The cremation ground is situated on the south-western part, a short distance from the village. The burial ground of the Mohammedan groups is located on the banks of the pond.

The village is divided into *mohallas* or wards composed of members of separate castes. The remarkable feature is that most of the high castes are concentrated in the central part of the village but occasionally construct their houses in the *mohallas* of other castes, while the lower castes rarely do so. Broadly, the Kachhi and Dhakar live in the north-eastern sector, the Mali at both ends of the main street running north-south, the Balai, Khatik and Muslims in the south-western sector, the Khati and Mogya in the north-western sector and the Bhangi in the eastern sector.

The village is not on level ground and consequently the houses are situated on uneven footing. Land surrounding the village is very valuable. The nucleus of the village has become particularly expensive because it simultaneously provides space for shops and meeting spots. High yields of crops bringing fair prices have impelled people to use every inch of land.

The houses in Awan have no definite pattern, but broadly they may be classified into three categories: large double-storeyed houses, smaller single-storeyed houses, and small huts.

The type of house depicts the status of the family. The large double-storeyed houses invariably have five or more rooms with a large compound or open courtyard and a roofed entrance. They are known as *pakka* houses. Both the places are used as cattle-sheds, one side of the latter or a cell at the first floor being used as a store-room for fuel cakes and cow-dung, and the other for grain, agricultural implements and spare parts of bullock carts. A corner of the courtyard is used for draining purposes. A stone slab is placed where the women take their bath. The courtyard is used for erecting a *mandap* at the time of marriages. Guests assemble in such courtyards during festive and ceremonial occasions. One of the rooms on the first floor is assigned to lodge the gods and deities invoked during a marriage. The rooms of the upper floor are used for cooking, living, and sleeping purposes. The verandahs are in front of the rooms and become a sort of entrance to them. The houses of the Hindus have a special place for the sacred *tulsi* plant which is watered daily after the worship of the gods and the sun. The upper side of the entrance often has a place for Ganesh, also called Vinayak, a deity that is supposed to be the remover of all obstacles. The doors of such houses are usually decorated with geometrical designs and engravings of human and animal figures. The walls are plastered and the floors are made of stone slabs or are coated with coloured earth and cow-dung. Muslims, leather working castes and untouchables have not been able to afford such marks of sophistication. Large windows, ventilation and other sanitation equipment apparently reflect urban influences. The entrance is flanked by two small platforms, called *gokharas* and *chuntara* or *chabutaras*. At some places the houses have an adjacent *nohra* (a courtyard with a cattle-shed) where large feasts are arranged during marriages.

Dari, jajam or *fursh* are used for furnishing the floor. Wooden furniture is meagre. Crude benches, chairs and stools and a large rectangular platform known as *takht*, supported on four legs, are the popular items. Bedsteads are of two types, the sophisticated *palang* and the simple *khat* or *charpoy*. The first is woven with cotton woven strips known as *nivar*, the second with hemp ropes. These seats, on which a carpet is spread, are provided for guests. Cheap prints of Hindu gods and deities or photographs taken at the weekly market or fair decorate the panels of the walls in some houses. The decorative designs, scenes from religious scriptures

and objects of modern communications and paintings of animals
and birds decorate the walls during the weddings.

Trousers, sport shirts, and open collar coats are worn by people
who have received some education. Some occasionally wear
inexpensive ties as well. City-made shoes are often used while
visiting the townships. Wrist watches, self-inking pens and sun
glasses are considered to be prestigious, sophisticated, urban
articles. In such houses metal utensils, usually of brass, are used
more often than any others. Some cheap crockery is also seen.
Food and water are served in brass plates and glass tumblers.

The second type of houses are single-storeyed and relatively
simple. They are constructed with stone and mud and plastered
with clay. The walls are white-washed. These belong to the
middle class. Such houses have a corridor, one or two verandahs, three to four rooms, and a courtyard. The roof is either
constructed of clay shingles, or stone slabs covered with sand
and lime plaster. Some roofs are covered with stone slabs or
indigenous clay tiles. In this group, those houses which are
coated with lime and sand or cement are known as *pakka*, and
those plastered with clay, straw, cow-dung, and white washed are
called *kaccha*.

The third category of houses are merely huts whose walls are
made of stones and plastered with brown clay and cow-dung.
These are often constructed by the dwellers themselves. Sometimes walls are made only of mud. Very often houses are not
equipped with latrines and the backyards are occasionally used
as improvised latrines. The roofs are made of reeds, rushes
and indigenous tiles. These require repairs every year before
the rainy season, the festival season of Diwali, and at the occasion
of marriages. The women of the family do the plastering while
the men take care of repairing the roofs. The people of meagre
economic means, usually belonging to lower and untouchable
castes, have such dwellings. During marriages the yard is used
for all ceremonies.

Temples and Abodes of Other Spiritual Powers

The presence of a temple particularly established by a caste
is indicative of the strength of the caste organisation. There
are fourteen temples in the village, eight maintained exclusively by different castes. The remaining six temples which do

not have any caste affiliation look practically deserted. The number of ruined temples bears witness to the prosperity of the village in the past.

The temples are consecrated to the greater gods and deities with a national character, such as Ram, Vishnu, Shankar or Mahadeo, Hanuman and Ganesh. The remains of temples of the *Tirthankars* are found in the village. The images of deities are brought from outside and installed with a ceremony called *padhrana*. Rejuvenation of temples is known as *doraferana*, which is followed by an elaborate feast embracing the people of caste from the *chokhala*, an inter-village organisation of caste. The temples are classified into several categories in relation to their ownership and management by different caste groups.

Besides the temples of the gods of Hinduism there are shrines and abodes of local deities. They are lodged over raised platforms beneath trees and at the wells. Most of the images are crude and locally made. There are oracles of these divinities belonging often to the castes of their followers. Among the main female deities are *Dudia-kheri-ki-Mataji*, *Sitala-mata*, *Lal-mata*, *Mari-mata*, and among the male ones, *Bheruji*, *Thakursaheb*, *Sagasji*, *Tejaji*, *Goraji*, *Bholaji*, *Jindji*, and *Shyamaji*. The last is the main deity of the Bhangi untouchables. Most of the caste associated temples are situated in the localities of their castes, but small shrines are unevenly distributed around the village. Most of the deities are invoked at times of illness and crisis. The *bhopa* (the oracle), the attendant of the deity, is possessed with the spirit of the deity when invoked. He reveals the unknown and mystical dictums connected with the situations. All female deities are worshipped and offered sacrifices during the *nauratha* (nine days) preceding the Dashahra celebrations. Propitiation includes prayers, worship and vows of faith.

Certain spots, such as ruined palaces, ponds, large trees, crematoriums and graveyards are considered to be haunted by profane spirits and dissatisfied souls of the dead. People fear visiting these spots alone or at late hours.

The Village and its Administrative Links

Awan can be reached by road via Kota, the district headquarters. The nearest railway station is Darah, located fifteen miles from Awan on the broad-gauge line which connects Delhi and Bombay. The village is so located that it has direct links with the cultural centres of Uttar Pradesh and the Malwa sub-region of Madhya Pradesh.

The weekly *hat* (market day) held on Sunday attracts people from ten to fifteen villages for several kinds of business transactions.

Thirty years ago Awan had no school. After Independence, a primary school was established which lately developed to the Higher Secondary level in 1959. An ayurvedic dispensary began functioning in 1954. However, it could not meet the needs of the people. The Primary Health Centre was established in 1965.

The village has the offices of *patwari*, village level worker, forest guard and Head Constable. District and divisional officers of the revenue, police, forest and development departments occasionally visit the village. The *grampanchayat* and the *nyay-panchayat* function as village and inter-village civil and judicial councils to deal with disputes connected with land, property and marriage.

As Edmund Leach has pointed out, the essence of the caste system lies in interrelationship among the castes (1960 : 5). Kingsley Davis considers the Hindu caste system the most thorough attempt in human history to institutionalise inequality (1949: 364). Srinivas also considered hierarchy as the chief ingredient of the caste system (1962).

THE VARNA THEORY

The *varna* system provides easy reference categories for locating the position of castes in the social hierarchy. The number of *varnas* has been changing. During the Rigveda period there were only two *varnas*, the Arya—the fair-skinned—and the Dasuya, the dark-skinned (cf. Apte 1954: 1-2). The present *varna* system comprises the Brahmin, the priests and the people of learning, the Kshatriya, the rulers and the warriors, and the Vaisya, the traders. The first three groups are regarded as *dwij* (twice-born) which symbolises spiritual rebirth and entitles a male belonging to these groups to undergo the *upnayan* or *janeu sanskar*. As an initiation rite it always precedes the marriage of a boy. This prescribes the wearing of *janeu*, the sacred thread. The fourth *varna*, i.e., Sudra, includes all cultivators, occupational and serving castes, who serve the castes belonging to the upper three *varnas* (see Table 1).

There are several myths and variations of stories of the creation of the *varna* system in the sacred books of Hinduism, but the one frequently repeated and accepted is the famous Purush myth of the Rigveda (about 1000 B.C.). The account refers to the creation of four classes arising from the body of the great god, Purush, viz., the Brahmin from the mouth, the Kshatriya from the arms, the Vaisya from the thighs and the Sudra from the feet.

Table I

(Figures against caste names indicate number of families)

Varna		Caste		
1. Brahmin	I	Brahmin 44 (Priestly occupations and landowners)		
2. Kshatriya	II	Rajput 16 (Landowners and cultivators)		
3. Vaisya	III	Mahajan 15 (Landowners and traders)		
4. Sudra	IV	Kayastha 3 (Landowners and record-keepers)	Khatri 3 (Landowners and money-lenders)	Sikh 4 (Landowners and money-lenders)
	V	Ahir (Pastoralists and agriculturists)	Dhakar 43 (Agriculturists)	Gujar 2 (Pastoralists)
		Mali 53 (Gardners & vegetable producers)	Kachhi 145 (Agriculturists)	
	VI	Darjee 4 (Tailors) — Khati 5 (Carpenters)	Sunar 4 (Goldsmiths)	Luhar (Blacksmiths)
		Tamoli 4 (Betel producers) — Kumhar 8 (Potters)	Teli 7 (Oil-massagers)	Patwa 2 (Thread-workers)
		Lakhara 1 (Lac bangle-makers)	Nai 5 (Barbers)	
	VII	Gosain 1 (Temple keepers)	Bairagi 4 (Religious mendicants)	Nath 3 (Temple keepers)
		Chhipa 1 (Weavers) — Kharwal 2 (Watchmen)	Rao 2 (Minstrels)	Kalal 3 (Distillers and liquor sellers)
		Dholi (Drummer)	Kumaravat 1 (Stone-workers)	Dhobi 6 (Washermen)
	VIII	Mogya 5 (Mat-makers)	Meena 1 Bhil 1 Nayak 2 (Tribal-castes)	
		Bavar 1 (folk doctors)	Khatik 16 (Butchers)	
	IX	Balai 52 (Weavers, masons and leather-tanners)		
		Mer 9 (Leather-tanners) — Bola 5 (Skinners)	Bhangi 5 (Sweepers)	

However, the so-called untouchables of the latter ages now occupy a position beneath the Sudra and are often included in the Sudra category.

The people of Awan offer several explanations as to why some castes are regarded as high and others as low. Yet most of the villagers agree that the Brahmin, Rajput, and Mahajan should be ranked higher in order of precedence. One of their sources of information is the *katha vachaks* (sacred story-tellers) who read to them from the stories of the sacred texts. The people's beliefs have also come from their knowledge of sacred scriptures, performance of rituals, and maintenance of purity-pollution norms. Members of the lower castes treat all upper caste members with equal respect, regardless of their social or economic position. Ritually, to a Balai leather-worker it makes little difference whether the Brahmin he is dealing with is a wealthy landowner or an impoverished priest.

The *varna* system gives us an understanding of a categorical classification depicted by the great tradition of Hinduism. The *varna* system does not fix the rank of a caste since a single *varna* applies to groups of castes and, therefore, the *varna* scheme operates broadly to suggest categories of castes on the basis of shared status, historical origins, life styles, and ritual behaviours (Fox 1969: 28). In the past *varna* served to rank classes of castes by status when fluidity in society was relatively greater (Weber 1958 : 55-56). Mandelbaum remarks: "Each *varna* is a reference category, a taxonomic device which does not denote a functioning group of cooperating people nor much in the way of cultural homogeneity." (Mandelbaum 1960: 442).

Recognising the limitations of the *varna* scheme, Mandelbaum has further pointed out that it omits those who rank below Sudras and that some *varna* categories are only sporadically represented in certain parts of India. However, the *varna* scheme continues to serve several purposes: (*i*) the scheme provides a simple way of indicating the sector of the hierarchy into which a particular *jati* can be fitted; (*ii*) it is a useful index of rank within a local system and a convenient scale to assess the rank of subcastes and castes of different regions; (3) it helps legitimise the higher rank claims of corporate groups who are trying to improve their social status (Mandelbaum

1960; also Mayer 1956: 138).

To summarise the above discussion, it is suggested that: (*i*) The *varna* scheme is a means to delineate broader categorisation of Hindu society. It provides, at least theoretically, a convenient scale to tentatively rank a caste in the social order of Hindu society at various levels. (*ii*) Since it is an omnibus scheme, one of its major functions is to set role expectations for those caste categories which have found a place in its fold. (*iii*) Broadly speaking, it suggests normative standards of interactions at various levels of the hierarchy among the members of castes and subcastes.

The exchange of food and water is strictly governed by well established traditions of the caste system. *Kaccha* food, which is prepared by roasting, may not be eaten by a person if it has been prepared by someone of a lower caste than his own. If a lower caste person enters the kitchen during the preparation of *kaccha* food, the food becomes "polluted" and is considered unacceptable. The rules pertaining to *pakka* food, which is fried, are more lenient. *Pakka* food makes it possible for the middle castes to invite the upper castes to their feasts and dinners. Apart from the *dwij* castes, others do not differentiate much between *kaccha* and *pakka* while dealing among themselves. They take note of these distinctions in relation to higher castes.

The rules regarding the acceptance of drinking water from a particular individual correspond to the rules for food. The higher castes do not accept water from clay vessels used by the lower castes for domestic purposes. A clay vessel filled with water, if touched by a Bhangi or Chamar, is thought to be polluted for all clean castes. The members of the first six divisions of castes can accept water from each other, except the Teli from whom Brahmin and Mahajan do not accept water. The women of clean artisan and agricultural groups of castes can offer water to higher castes. Nobody in the higher caste groups would take water from the groups belonging to leather-working castes and the untouchables. Water kept in leather containers is not accepted by the Brahmin, Mahajan, Darjee, Khati, Sunar, Tamboli, Luhar and Teli, but the rest of the castes accept water from the well drawn in leather *charas*. Theoretically, if the members of castes can receive water from another caste, they can also receive *pakka* food from them.

CASTE GROUPS IN THE VILLAGE

The Brahmin

Ritual pre-eminence of the Brahmin is ascertained by their knowledge of the scriptures and sacred practices. They occupy an indisputable position at the top of the caste hierarchy. Traditionally the Brahmins are known as priests, teachers, religious mendicants and ascetics, but now they are also landlords, money-lenders, and businessmen. They drink no liquor and are strict vegetarians.

The Brahmins, who are devoted to their traditional calling, are generally expected to be well-versed in the knowledge of the sacred texts. As priests and teachers they officiate at sacred rites and ceremonies for which they receive alms and gifts. Wealthy Brahmins neither work as priests nor administer ritual ministrations, and are often accused of failing to maintain the scholarly standard for which their caste is known. Ritual purity is not based on intellectual abilities, but rather upon conduct in accordance with scriptural rules of purity.

Scriptural injunctions provide support for their ritual purity, yet their interactions with other villagers are largely influenced by secular considerations. Application of the ritual criteria sets broader limits within which a caste or subcaste can be ranked. Claims for supremacy by a subcaste within the framework of the caste are derived from historical antecedents and are strongly influenced by the wealth and power of its members. Thus, ritual criteria suggests formal precedence, though the actual influence might be little. Moreover, the ritual dominance of the Brahmin caste does not automatically provide the Brahmin with economic or political power.

The Rajput

The Rajputs, traditionally known as rulers and warriors, are ranked just below the Brahmins in the caste hierarchy. They belong to the Kshatriya *varna*. The Rajputs are respected by all the castes for their glamorous heritage. The 16 households of the Rajputs in Awan do not belong to the ruling class. They engage primarily in agricultural occupations, and as such are not an influential group. Awan was not a *jagirdari* (feudal) village, so the Rajputs have not enjoyed the privileges and enhanced prestige of the princely rulers. The Rajputs are considered to be ancient inhabitants of the village and their history is mingled with mythology. In the recent past they played no important part in the administration of the village. All the families belong to the three major exogamous clans—the Solanki, Chauhan and Kachhavah. They accept *kaccha* food from all the castes except Kumarawat, Dhobi, Mogya, Bavar, Meena, Bhil, Nayak, Balai, Mer, Bola and Bhangi, and *pakka* from the hands of all the castes except the Dhobi, the leather-working castes and the Bhangi. The Rajputs are non-vegetarians, but their meat diet is limited to mutton, pork and chicken.

The Mahajan

The Mahajan or Bania rank below the Rajput. They claim supremacy over the Rajput because of their vegetarianism, their abstinence from alcohol and their economic success. Most Mahajans are traders, money-lenders and landowners, and most cloth, grocery and general merchandise shops in Awan are owned by them. The seven subcastes of the Mahajans are classified into three religious sects, viz., the Vaishnavaite comprising the Maheshwari, Agrawal and the Chittora; the Vaishnavaite-cum-Jain comprising the Vijayvargiya, the Khandelwal and the Porwal; and the Jain comprising the Oswal. All castes except the Brahmin accept *kaccha* food from them. They do not accept *kaccha* food from any caste whose ritual position is lower than their own. They also refuse food from the Rajputs because of their non-vegetarian food habits and acceptance of *kaccha* food from a large number of lower castes from whom the Mahajan do not accept *kaccha* food.

The Kayastha

The Kayastha are traditionally known as scribes and are often associated with offices of the state. They rank next to the Mahajan group but are non-vegetarian. Awan has only three families of Kayastha, only one of which has a standing of thirty years in the village. The other two are the households of the teachers employed in the government school. The Kayastha accept *kaccha* food from all the castes except the leather-working castes and the untouchables.

Khatri-Sikh

The Khatri and the Khatri-Sikh are immigrants from the Punjab who arrived in the village nearly thirty years ago. They are landowners, money-lenders and flour-mill owners. They are non-vegetarian and accept *kaccha* food from all castes except the leather-workers and untouchables. Occasionally they drink liquor. Their ritual position in the village is disputable. While they place themselves on level with the Rajput, the villagers consider them much lower.

THE AGRICULTURAL CASTES

Although most of the castes in the village are landowners, not all of them are cultivators. The castes of division 5 (Table 1) are primarily agriculturists. Most of their members drink liquor and eat all meats except beef. They are generally rugged and uneducated.

The Ahir

The seven households of Ahirs farm and raise sheep, cows and buffaloes for a living. They are ranked a little higher than other agricultural castes and are traditionally known as herdsmen who rear cows, buffaloes, and sell milk and *ghee*. Since they own few cattle they work as croppers, watchman, *halis* (contractual servants), etc. The Ahir caste *panchayat* embraces five villages within a five-mile circumference. They accept *kaccha* food from all agricultural castes except from those who are ranked below the Gosain. *Pakka* food is accepted by them from all the castes except the leather-working and untouchable castes.

The Dhakar

The Dhakar are primarily small landowners and farmers. The caste *panchayat* of the Dhakar is a well-organised group which maintains the caste rules prescribed by the local council. Inter-dining at feasts with the Ahir, the Gujar, and the Mali is common among the Dhakar. The two endogamous groups of Dhakar, the Nagar Dhakar and Mali Dhakar, trace their origin from the Rajput and hence follow the latter's pattern to some extent. They have been influenced by the Brahmin and the Mahajan caste groups and have borrowed some of their marriage rites from them, such as the distribution of *tai* and the offering of *dhwaja* at the temple. The endogamous character of the sub-castes has not been strictly maintained and there have been marriages between the members of the two groups. The *kaccha* food is accepted from all castes above the Gosain and *pakka* from the castes above the Khatik.

The Gujar

The Gujars are farmers who also rear buffaloes and cows. There are only two families of Gujars in the village. They associate themselves with the Ahir and the Dhakar for all func-tional purposes of the caste. For caste activities they join their fellow caste members who live in the surrounding villages. The Gujars have a ritual ranking equal to the Ahir, the Dhakar, and the Mali, and are considered a little superior to the Kacchi. Their intercaste activities follow a pattern similar to that of the Dhakar.

The Mali

The Mali caste, which is said to be a descendant of the Rajputs, can be divided into three groups: the Fuleria Mali, the Kachhi Mali, and the Dheemar Mali. Of the fifty-three Mali families in Awan most are professional gardeners and farmers but the Dheemar Mali are boatsmen and water suppliers.

The Fuleria Mali and Dheemar Mali live in the northern and southern sectors of the village respectively and own two meeting houses known as Mali bungalows. They are used for feasts, meetings, and marriage parties. Their ritual status in the hierarchy is almost equal to the Dhakar and a little higher than the Kachhi. The Kachhi, however, do not recognise the Mali's superiority.

The Kachhi

Of all the agricultural castes, the Kachhi, with 145 households and nearly 27 per cent of the village population, are the most predominant. They are basically cultivators who also work as labourers, croppers, and watchmen. The Kachhi neighbourhood is in the north-eastern sector of the village with two caste temples in its nucleus. Like other agricultural castes who have sought links with the ruling Rajput lineages, they consider themselves the descendants of some Kachhava Rajput ruler of Jaipur.

The Kachhi have an active caste *panchayat* which embraces

the local population of the village and another village located in the vicinity. Due to the large membership of the caste, the Kachhi rarely seek assistance from other castes on their ritual occasions, except for the traditional services from the Brahmin priest, Nai, Dhobi and Bhangi. The caste council is administered by a *bada patel* (headman), five *patels* (the members) and a *kotwal* (the executive member). These officials not only deal with the breaches of the caste rules but also handle the ritual and economic activities of the caste. The Kachhi are the only people who do not allow their women to enter the sacred areas. They accept *kaccha* food from all the castes above the Gosain and *pakka* food from all the castes above the Khatik. If breaches of these rules are reported, the defaulter may be fined up to Rs 11. Such fines are collected and deposited in the treasury of the caste council.

THE ARTISAN CASTES

The Darjee

The four families of the Darjee are descendants of the oldest families of the village. They have their *satis* in the village belonging to the Tada clan of the Darjee. According to a popular myth the Darjee are said to have originated from the Brahmin, but this is not substantiated by any factual evidence. The members of this caste are traditionally known as tailors, but the introduction of sewing machines brought members of other castes such as the Brahmin, Kalal, and Muslims into the Darjee's trade. They accept *kaccha* food from only the Brahmin, the Mahajan and the Sunar. *Pakka* food is accepted from all the castes above the Kalal. The Darjee do not eat meat or drink liquor.

The Khati

The Khati is another group whose members are said to have originated from the Brahmin and hence they are also vegetarians and non-drinkers. Primarily, the Khati are carpenters who make agricultural implements, doors and windows, cots, tripods, bullock-carts and furniture. The Khati are relatively prosperous people who often own small pieces of land. The Khati supply the *manda* rods and *torans* for the marriages of all castes. Their homes are scattered throughout the north-western and north-eastern sectors of the village. The Khati accept *kaccha* food from all the castes ranked above them, except the Kumhar, the Luhar, the Sunar, the Tamoli and the Teli, who are ranked with them in matters of social intercourse. *Pakka* food is accepted from all the castes above the Kalal.

The Sunar

The Sunar are professional goldsmiths who manufacture gold and silver ornaments. The four families of goldsmiths all own some land and also lend money to their customers. The Sunar accept *kaccha* food from all the castes ranked above the Gosain and *pakka* food from the castes above the Kalal. On many ritual occasions they imitate the customs of the Brahmin and the Mahajan caste groups. The Sunar are an economically prosperous group who live in the locality of the twice-born castes. This proximity, along with their clean occupation and vegetarianism, have brought them much closer to the Brahmin and the Mahajan.

The Luhar

Twice a year, during the tilling and harvest seasons, the six Luhar households engage in their traditional profession of making and repairing tools and agricultural implements. The Luhar women assist in handling the bellows at the forge. Their customers pay them in cash or kind at the end of the harvest each year. The Luhar are vegetarians. *Kaccha* food is accepted by them from all the castes ranked above the Gosain and *pakka* from all the castes placed above the Dhobi.

The Tamboli

Originally the Tamboli were betel growers and sellers. They had decorative shops which displayed looking-glasses and inexpensive calendars. Of the four Tamboli families in Awan only one is engaged in the traditional business. The other three have become *halwais* (confectioners). They neither eat meat nor drink liquor. They are employed as cooks for marriage feasts. The Tamboli are ranked equally with the Khati, and their acceptance of food and water is determined by the same rules as those of the Khati.

The Kumhar

The Kumhar make pots and occasionally bricks and tiles. Their women supply water to the higher and clean castes. The kilns for baking the pots and tiles are known as *say* and are located near their houses. The Kumhar also rear donkeys, which are the main carriers of loads. The villagers gossip about the Kumhars' excessive drinking habits and claim that most of their money is spent on liquor during marriages, caste meetings, and even weekly market days. Supplying earthern pots and ceremonial *basan* (clay-pot sets) to the *yajman* or *jajman* is the chief duty of the Kumhar. Each year they receive 5 to 10 kilograms of grain during the crop season for their work. Because they are suspected of eating meat the Kumhar are ranked beneath the Khati and Darjee. They accept *kaccha* food from all the castes ranked above the Kalal.

The Teli

All seven Teli households in Awan earn their living by pressing linseed or sesame oil, the traditional occupation of the caste. However, some have taken up secondary occupations such as selling groceries or raising cows and buffaloes. A caste council which covering twenty villages handles major decisions such as breaches of caste regulations, problems relating to remarriage, and the basic organisation of the caste. The Teli are regarded as "clean", but the Brahmin and the Mahajan do not accept water from them. However, in other parts of southern Rajasthan, the Teli serve as cooks for *pakka* food during marriages. By refraining from meat and liquor they follow the example of the Brahmin and Mahajan groups even though they are said to have descended from the Kshatriya. The Teli accept *kaccha* food from all castes higher than the Bairagi and *pakka* food from those higher than the Balai.

The Patwa

The Patwa are needle-workers who decorate ornaments with gaudy silver and gold designs. They also sell inexpensive cosmetics. The Patwa sell their wares in the neighbouring villages on *hat* (weekly market) days and during seasonal fairs. They also offer *bandarvals* (decorative thread-work) for doors on the occasions of births and marriages. The Patwa women occasionally supply water to the twice-born castes. They accept *kaccha* food from all the castes higher than them except the Kumhar, the Luhar and the Teli, and *pakka* food from all the castes ranked above the Balai. They are vegetarians who occasionally drink liquor, although it is prohibited by caste norms.

The Lakhara

Among the other artisan castes, the Lakhara, whose traditional occupation is making lac bangles, has only one family in the village. The Lakhara have a shop which the women of Awan and the neighbouring villages visit occasionally. The city-made bangles of lac are remoulded to the size needed by the customers. Festive occasions attract a large number of customers. The Patwa are a clean caste of vegetarians and non-drinkers. They accept *kaccha* food from all the castes ranked above them in the hierarchy save the Kumhar and the Luhar, and *pakka* food from all those ranked higher than the Balai.

The Nai

The Nai are the barbers of the village. Their women are nurses and midwives for women of the clean castes. They also prepare *pattals* and *done* (leaf-plates and cups) for festive occasions. The Nai are the most important of all the *kamins* (the serving castes). They are hired by all castes above the Balai to arrange and handle the ritual feasts and ceremonies for marriages, births and deaths. Their duties also include giving haircut, shaves and massages to the members of the family employing them. They also wash the familys' clothes, clean the house, attend to guests at their baths, and run any errands which might be necessary. The extent of the services rendered by the Nai varies with the status of the caste they are serving. They are paid between 10 to 30 kilograms of *gava* (corn) a year by their *jajmans*. Occasionally, they also receive gifts of clothing, food or money. The Nai accept *kaccha* food from all the castes ranked above the Kumarawat and *pakka* from all castes ranked above the Balai. The Nai are a "clean" caste and the twice-born castes accept water and *pakka* food served by them.

SECTARIAN CASTES

The Gosain

The Gosain, Bairagi and the Nath are comprised exclusively of temple keepers and mendicants of different sects. Therefore, they have been labelled sectarian castes. The one family of Gosain in the village is Vaishanavite. The Gosain claim they rank next to the Brahmin in the hierarchy of castes, but other castes rank them below the castes of division 6, since the Brahmin and Mahajan do not accept water from them.

The Bairagi

The Bairagi have four families and claim to have the longest history in the village. A *bairagi* (one who has renounced worldy life) as a member of any caste is to be distinguished from a person belonging to the Bairagi caste. They belong to the Saiva sect of Hinduism. Some of the persons who had earlier adopted the *bairagi* pattern of life but later married and turned *sansari* (worldly) were instrumental in the formation of this caste. In Awan, no such instance of renunciation has been reported during the last fifty years. The Bairagi accept gifts of corn from all castes except the Bhangi, and *kaccha* food from all castes except those ranked below them. *Pakka* food is accepted from all castes ranked above the Kumarawat. The Bairagi look after the temple of Lord Siva, belonging to the Khatik.

The Nath

One of the ancient sacred spots in the village is the *math*, known as *Nathon-ka-math*, in which the image of Lord Siva was installed by some Nath celibate a few hundred years ago. It is said that the founder of the temple had taken *bhumi-samadhi*, i.e. buried himself alive. His disciple took charge of the *math*. Four generations ago the temple keeper married a *sansarin*, a woman of the non-celibate endogamous group of the Nath caste. The existing three families are the descendants of the temple keeper, and one of them maintains the temple with the economic assistance from the fifteen bighas of land allotted as *doli* (rent-free land) in the name of the *math*. The other two families are agriculturists. The Naths have abandoned begging, but accept alms, charity, foodstuffs and other offering presented at the *math*. They receive *seedha*, a plate of raw foodstuffs offered on *Poornima*, *Amavasya* and other festival days, from the clean castes. The Nath accept *kaccha* food from all the castes ranked above them, save the Kumhar, the Luhar and the Teli. They accept *pakka* food from all the castes placed above the Khatik, excluding the Dhobi and the Mogya.

The Chhipa

The Chhipa are traditional weavers, but the one family in Awan has adopted agriculture as its main occupation. They eat mutton and pork and enjoy liquor at times. They accept *kaccha* food from all the castes above the Kumarawat, and *pakka* food from all those above the Balai. The Chhipa have a large population in the nearby villages who practise their traditional occupation.

The Kharwal

The Kharwal collect *khar* (saline products) from local sources. They also work as watchmen and croppers on the fields of other castes. They have no caste council since there are only two families in the village. The Kharwal accept *kaccha* food from all the castes above the Kumarawat and *pakka* from all those above the Balai (cf. Briggs 1920: 32).

The Rao

The two Rao families in the village are the genealogists of the Mali. Supposedly all castes have a caste genealogist but only seven actually do. Since the Rao are wholly dependent upon their traditional occupation, they go from house to house on Mali ritual occasions to obtain gifts of corn. During a Mali marriage, the Rao sing folk songs in praise of the caste. The Rao accept *kaccha* food from all castes ranked above the Khatik, excluding the Dhobi, Mogya and the Bavar, and *pakka* food from all those ranked above the Balai.

The Kalal

Traditionally the Kalal are the caste who distil and sell liquor. Disitlling and selling of liquor is now permissible if a licence has been obtained from the government. At present there is only one Kalal shop which sells liquor.   They are considered relatively untouchable by the Brahmin, the Mahajan, the Darjee, the Khati and the Sunar.   The Kalal accept *kaccha* as well as *pakka* food from all castes ranked above them, the degree of interaction being less with castes lower than their own.   They have been trying to improve their ritual status by becoming vegetarians.   Most of them have chosen secular occupations like tailoring, teaching and book-keeping.

The Kumarawat

The Kumarawat as a caste are known as masons, but the one Kumarawat family in Awan farms for a living.   The Kumarawat are said to have originated from the Balai, but consider themselves higher than the Balai because they have abandoned the Balai's traditional occupation of leather tanning.   The Kumarawat accept *kaccha* food from all castes ranked above them, excluding the Chhipa, Kharwal, the Rao and the Kalal, and *pakka* food from all castes ranked above the Balai.

The Dhobi

Awan's six families of Dhobi clean laundry for a living.   Since they are willing to wash clothes soiled by human emissions, their occupation and caste are considered polluted.   Devout members of the twice-born castes will not wear clothes washed by the Dhobi while worshipping the gods.   The Dhobi are non-vegetarians who eat mutton and pork.   They are known to be heavy drinkers who serve liquor at all ritual occasions.   The Dhobi accept *kaccha* food from all castes ranked above them except the Dhobi, Kharwal, Chhipa, Rao and the Kumarawat, and *pakka* food from all castes ranked above the Balai.

The Mogya

The Mogya have five households in the north-eastern sector of the village.   They are considered untouchables by all the clean castes since they make mats, fans, baskets, bamboo-carriers and brooms from the leaves of palm trees.   Due to the seasonal nature of their occupation, the Mogya also have taken jobs as croppers, watchmen and contractual servants.   They occasionally eat mutton and drink liquor.   The Mogya accept *kaccha* food from any caste above them, save the Dhobi, and *pakka* food from all except the leather-working castes and the Bhangi.

The Bhil, Meena and Nayak

The four families of the tribal castes belong to the Meena, Bhil and Nayak. The Meena consider themselves a little higher and purer than their two associates from whom they are said to have originated. The tribal castes are known as "unclean" groups and therefore "clean" castes do not accept water from them. However, in the Udaipur district of Rajasthan the tribes with synonymous names are considered pure and clean. All these people are engaged in agricultural activities. They accept *kaccha* food from all the castes ranked above them except the Kumarawat, the Dhobi and the Mogya. They accept *kaccha* food from the Khatik who are ranked below them. *Pakka* food is accepted from all the castes ranked above the Balai.

The Bavar

The Bavar and his two wives are the only people in Awan who practise folk medicine. The wives act as midwives for all castes except the untouchables. The male Bavar is able to relieve soreness and stiffness from minor injuries through an operation called *singi*. He pricks the afflicted area of the body several times with a heavy pin, applies a horn pipe, and sucks blood from the hole. It is believed that the cause of the problem is blocked, stagnant blood and that the Bavar will extract only the harmful dead blood. He also sets bones by massaging and sells various indigenous medicines. They supplement their curative therapy with magico-religious practices and witchcraft. The Bavar eat meat and drink liquor. They accept *kaccha* food from all castes ranked above them excluding the Dhobi and the Mogya, and *pakka* food from all castes ranked above the Balai.

The Khatik

The breeding, butchering, and selling of goats and sheep is the traditional occupation of the Khatik. Lately some have also begun trading wool. Nine of the sixteen families in Awan have adopted farming as their major occupation. The Khatik eat meat, drink liquor, and accept food from any caste ranked above them except the Dhobi and the Mogya.

THE LEATHER-WORKERS AND UNTOUCHABLE GROUPS

The Balai

The Balai, the Mer and the Bola are traditionally tanners and skinners. All of them are referred to under the common term *chamar*. Awan's Balai caste comprises 15 weavers, 17 masons and 20 agriculturists, all of whom abandoned the occupation of leather tanning long ago. They are known as *Jhangara* Balai. Some of them have reportedly stopped drinking liquor and eating beef and carrion. As an effort to upgrade their position they have begun using the suffix *jatava*, a colloquial form of *yadava*, as their surname indicating descendancy from a popular Rajput clan. They frequently share meals with the Mer and the Bola, but intermarriages are discouraged to maintain the superiority of their caste. The Balai accept food from all the castes ranked above them, except the Dhobi and the Mogya, whom they consider unclean castes.

The Mer

The nine families of Mer are said to have split from the Balai, They refer to a myth that claims they descended from a *rishi's* wife, who gave birth to a set of twins in a field. The one who was delivered in the middle of the field was known as Balai and the other who was delivered at the *mer* (boundary) was called Mer Balai. The Mer are primarily agriculturists who rear goats as a subsidiary vocation. They also deal in hides and skins at weekly markets and fairs. The women bring wood and leaves from the forest and sell them in the village lanes. The Balai consider themselves superior to the Mer, but the latter do not accept this ranking. They accept *kaccha* as well as *pakka* food from all the castes ranked above them.

The Bola

Among the leather-working castes, the Bola are ranked the lowest. The five families of Bola skin animals, tan leather and make indigenous shoes. The women collect herbs from the forest for tanning leather. The men and women both sew colourful designs on shoes with silver thread. The shoes are sold at weekly markets and fairs held in the surrounding villages. Eating beef and carrion and drinking liquor is common among the Bola. Along with leather-work, the Bola are cultivators, croppers and tenants. They are considered so low that the barbers refuse to cut their hair, forcing them to cut their own.

The Bola used to give half of the hide of the dead cattle to the owner and received 2 to 5 kilograms of grains for removing the carcass. Now they charge Rs 2 to Rs 5 for this service and return no hide to the owner. Interdining with the Balai and the Mer is permitted on the occasion of marriages and funerals.

The Bhangi

The Bhangi are the untouchables who are placed at the bottom of the hierarchy of castes. The five families of Bhangi have their houses in the north-eastern sector of the village, and are detached from the main locality. The Bhangi are scavengers who sweep the streets and latrines of all the castes, an activity which has earned them their undisputed position at the bottom.

The Bhangi accept scraps of food from the plates of the castes ranked above the Balai, save the Dhobi, the Dholi and the Mogya. They rear domestic pigs which are roasted before marriages for marriage parties and guests. Their use of liquor is quite frequent. Normally, a Bhangi receives food daily and some money monthly from his *jajmans* for sweeping their lanes. Occasionally old clothes and special food are given on the days of festivals. The Bhangi women receive *mangat* from the shopkeepers who set up their shops in the village street on weekly market days.

Although the Bhangi sweep the lanes and latrines of Muslims, they do not accept food from them. They accept monthly cash payment ranging from Re 0.50 to Re 1 from each family. The Bhangi claim that they are Hindus and cannot accept food from Muslims.

THE MUSLIM GROUPS

Besides the Hindu castes in Awan, there are other occupational groups who belong to the Sunni sect of the Mohammedan religion. Though the Muslims do not claim to have any caste-like hierarchy among themselves, the Hindu impact has given them a feeling of caste characteristics associated with occupations (cf. Dube, 1955a: 35). As such their occupation has become a factor in determining their position in their own social stratification. The Muslims are musicians, masons, gardeners, cultivators, croppers, tailors and teachers. On the basis of traditional occupations the Muslims may be grouped in the manner given below. Intermarriage among the six groups below is permissible but not preferred.

(The figure in parentheses indicates the number of families)

Momin (20) (masons)	Nilgar (5) (dyers)	Pinjara (2) (cotton-carders)
Julaha (1) (weavers)	Fakir (3) (religious mendicants)	Nat (1) (acrobats)

IRREGULAR SEXUAL UNIONS AND CASTE STATUS

Cases of illegal sexual unions are not openly discussed, but they do occur. Such unions, if discovered, bring disrepute to both parties. Cases involving Brahmin and Mahajan men becoming involved with women from leather-working castes or even untouchables have been reported. It is considered even more disgraceful when a lower caste male is associated with a woman of a higher caste. Children born out of wedlock bear the caste of the mother. The wives of unattractive men may become involved in affairs with men of other castes but their children are socially recognised as full members of the woman's husband's caste.

No case has been reported of a girl giving birth to a child through premarital relations, since girls are married before they approach puberty in most castes. If one is not, there are strict limitations on her activities until she is married. Illicit sexual intercourse between members of the lower castes has been reported, but this generally occurs between engaged couples and is not frequent.

chapter 4/Internal Structure of Castes

THE CASTES AND SUBCASTES

An analysis of the internal organisation of castes would reveal
the nature and workings of their various units. A caste cuts across
the physical boundaries of the village, and more often than not,
includes members spread across a number of villages. Much
has been written about ambiguities and inconsistencies in the
various usages of the words caste and subcaste. It may be
emphasised that these terms convey specific meanings depending
on the contexts of use. A caste is an endogamous, hereditary
social group which bears a name and an attributed ritual status
along with a set of distinctive characteristics (cf. Ghurye 1957:19).
The subcastes are usually endogamous groups within a caste
which often assume all the functions of a caste such as restricting
the choice of occupations, exercising civil and religious rights,
setting preferences for marital alliances, and assisting in certain
ritual and economic matters. Actually, there is a consistent
relationship between the all-encompassing nature of the caste
and its various units at different levels of operation in Indian
society. A person is bound to many other persons with multiple
strands. Within the caste he is linked with a subcaste, clan,
subclan, lineage, and family.

The term *jat biradari* refers to the two types of relationships
which link a person to these various groups. *Jat* or *jati* refers to
the sphere of families between which marriage is possible.
Biradari, the larger of the two groups, is a ritual brotherhood
which consists of a set of subcastes, an amorphous population
with unique traits and certain similarities. These groups are
formed with prospects of united action for religious, economic,
and political purposes.

While interdining among the members of different subcastes

is permissible, intermarriage is prohibited. J. H. Hutton has discerned that the segregation of the subcastes as part of a caste has been based upon intermarriage. When a subcaste accepts wives from other subcastes, while at the same time refusing to give daughters to such subcastes, it establishes its superiority over the others. This claim to superiority is generally based on a change of occupation (Hutton 1963: 51). However, this phenomenon is not supported by facts observed in Awan.

When a subcaste is not large enough to function as an independent organisation, a set of them is classed together under one name. These subcastes are usually similar in such respects as occupation, rank, and commensality. Formulation of a subcaste cluster leads to a formal organisation. Outside castes may make no distinction between the subcastes, but each subcaste holds itself socially apart from other subcastes of the cluster. Finer distinctions such as subcaste, lineage, and family are meaningful to the respective members only.

To maintain the purity of a caste or subcaste, its members are obligated to follow the caste rules governing the selection of mates. The rules of avoidance are dictated by the subcaste's organisation and are generally applicable to all its members throughout the region. Occasionally such rules are relaxed; when suitable mates are scarce due to regional peculiarities, one is forced to seek a partner outside the region. While such lapses do not establish a rule, they are taken into consideration by caste members while arranging future marriages.

CASTE AND SUBCASTE CLUSTERS

A common ritual rank of several castes or subcastes and a combination of shared attributes encourages them to join forces and share many of their activities. These groups, while classed together, are usually known by their individual characteristics, such as ritual rank, traditional occupation, and food habits. Every subcaste is spread over a number of villages in the region. Members of each are also governed by a common body, the subcaste council, which examines cases related to the breach of norms set for commensality and marriages.

Any subcaste which is so small that it is not economically, politically, and ritually self-sufficient finds itself in a very vulner-

able position. A large lower caste may attempt to withhold
services from a small higher caste to force its demands for higher
ritual recognition. The small higher caste may find its interest
unrepresented in the village council for lack of support. It
may find itself forced to seek ritual assistance from lower castes,
thereby compromising its own ritual position. By joining forces
with other subcastes of approximately the same standing, a
subcaste is able to eliminate many of the disadvantages of standing
alone. A subcaste is governed by rigid norms which dictate the
responsibilities each person has to the cluster. By assuming
these responsibilities a subcaste is also able to depend on cooperation and assistance from its fellow subcastes.

An example of such a cluster is that of the Brahmins of Awan,
whose forty-two families are distributed over six subcastes, viz.,
Dadhich 5, Gujargaur 6, Khandelwal 5, Sanadhya 9, Sriguar
6 and Sukhwal 11. Each of these groups is endogamous, the
members of each hold themselves socially apart from other subcastes of the same subcaste cluster. But to infuse a greater
sense of identity, these subcastes have formed a *jat panchayat*
(caste council) which handles disputes and breaches of caste
conduct codes. The *jat panchayat* also works to promote corporate action among the subcastes to obtain the common goals of
the cluster members.

Another function of the caste cluster is to bring together castes
and subcastes with similar occupations. The Mahajan (or Bania)
subcastes of the Vaishya *varna* have joined forces despite their
religious differences. Even though the seven families of the
Maheshwari subcaste and the single families of Chittora are
Vaishnava, and Oswal are Jain, while the two Agrawal families,
two Vijayavargiya families, and the single families of the Khandelwal and Porwal subcastes are Vaishnavites as well as Jain, traditionally these subcastes are known as traders, grocers, cloth
merchants and money lenders. The caste cluster attempts to keep
outsiders from entering their business and works to obtain any
benefits it can muster for the members of the cluster.

The membership in a caste cluster is not automatic. The
regional variations in caste practices are of paramount importance in determining membership in caste clusters. For example,
a Kashmiri or Bengali Brahmin is a non-vegetarian, which
contradicts the norms of the Brahmin in Awan. Therefore,

Awan's Brahmins feel superior to the Kashmiri or Bengali Brahmin and would not join a caste cluster with them.

A caste or subcaste cluster also may attempt to collectively justify its claim for a higher rank, usually by the group that is not twice-born. They cite appropriate myths and reinterpret various historical events to suit their position. Characteristically, such a cluster strengthens its attack by charging the upper castes with social oppression, claiming that its rights are being infringed upon and that it should stand strongly against such a menace. Whether or not such claims are considered genuine by other castes, united political and economic action is often effective.

The relations between united subcastes are not always harmonious. Political rivalries, conflicting personal interests, and even irregular attendance at important caste meetings cause altercations between the groups of the coalition. Often only a few men seeking personal gain are at the bottom of a major caste dispute. They may try to prevent a prestigious marriage or block a political bargain for a rival group in their caste cluster, While such splits are not quickly forgotten, they are rarely permanent due to the stabilising factor of shared formal rituals.

THE CLAN

A *gotra* or a clan is a unilateral group and the largest exogamous division of a caste or a subcaste. Membership in a clan hinges upon one line and, since Awan has all patrifamilies, the clan is traced through legendary patrilineal ancestors. Membership of the clan is usually dispersed throughout the region and sometimes beyond the region. Supposedly, it is a group which binds people from a great many villages. While it is rarely a corporate group in terms of holding common property, it tends to have common marriage regulations, rituals, and ceremonies concerning common deities (cf. Firth 1951: 35-36; Murdock 1949: 41; Radcliffe-Brown 1950: 39-40; Westermarck 1925: 52; Winick 1961: 18, 323-24).

Vansha or lineage is a group whose genealogical connections can be traced to a known common ancestor. In this sense a lineage is a body of people in which a common descent can be traced, while the clan is a larger group which embraces people who bear the same clan name, but with whom direct genealogical connections may not be traced out. Theoretically, the members of a clan relate themselves to a common ancestor, and therefore affinal ties among the members of a clan are considered to be incestuous.

Vansha and *kul* are synonymously used to refer to the agnatic line. Every *kul* is affiliated with the tutelary goddess and a complex of ritual activity. The goddess is known by different appellations such as *ghar-ki-devi, dehadi, mata, kul-mata, kul devi*. The Brahmin have different symbols, totems and ritual patterns within a single *gotra*-group whose members worship different *kul-devis* or *dehadis*. Such patterns are also prevalent in the Agrawal, the Vijayavargiya, and the Maheshwari Mahajan families. Among the Dhakar, the Kachhi, and the Mali, *dehadis* are equally significant.

The clan in turn includes the family and the local agnatic group. Such a dispersed membership of persons related through agnatic ties is linked to a common clan name which is derived from the name of some place, incident, tree, animal, person, spirit, deity, or physical appearance of the ancestor. The clan descends through patrilineal succession and shares an affiliation with the *dehadi* (the family goddess). Just as membership of a caste is not transferable, so also the membership of the clan is not transferable.

Clan is frequently used as a synonym for *sakha* (branch). A clan is subdivided into *khanps* (subclans) depending upon the worship of different *dehadis* or *kul-devis* (family goddesses) which usually derive their names from trees or grains. The members of the clan worship *dehadi* on *Ashtami*, which occurs twice a year, or on occasions allotted specially for her propitiation. It is also noted that the symbol, totem, and mode of worship are not usually the same of *dehadis* of different *gotra* groups.

After the marriage of a girl, she joins the clan of her husband. Her parents' clan still plays an important role in establishing the matrimonial alliances of her children. A clan functions as an exogamous category which helps to distinguish the prospective spouses from those who are ineligible.

Generally, in the region in which the marriage alliance is sought, the principles of *gotra* avoidance are strictly followed. Any breach is considered an anti-caste activity leading to ritual defilement. Such infractions are dealt with by the concerned caste or the subcaste council. According to north Indian ideals, an individual while finalising the marriage alliance should take into consideration the avoidance of the following four *gotras*: (*i*) *gotra* of the person, (*ii*) *gotra* of the mother (biological), (*iii*) *gotra* of the father's mother, and (*iv*) *gotra* of the mother's mother (cf. Karve 1965: 118).

The rule of *gotra* avoidance among the castes is not consistent with the hierarchy of the castes. For example, the Brahmin, the Mahajan, the Kumhar, the Teli, the Kalal, the Dhobi, the Balai and the Bhangi follow the four *gotra* avoidance rules, while the Rajput, the Kayastha, the Dhakar, the Mali, the Kachhi the Kalal and Khatik follow the three *gotra* avoidance principles. Among the Kachhi clan endogamy is practised to narrow the exogamous unit to a group associated with *dehadi*.

The castes ranked below the twice-born castes at the various levels of the hierarchy often make efforts to imitate the practices of the twice-born castes. The castes which attempt to imitate the Brahmin and the Mahajan way of life observe the four *gotra* avoidance rules, while those who have adopted the Kshatriya path have observed the three *gotra* avoidance rules.

THE LINEAGE

The *vansh* or lineage is a consanguine kin group whose members trace their origin unilaterally to a common ancestor. They are not necessarily expected to share a common locality (cf. Murdock 1949: 178; Winick 1961: 323). In Awan the people are patrilineal. Locally the lineage is considered to be a group consisting of members related in the prevalent line of descent through genealogical ties. The members are also expected to observe a set of common rituals, but not necessarily share a common household. The reputation of a person is determined by the reputation of his forbearers. For example, if a boy's grandfather had been wealthy and lived lavishly, the boy could become destitute and still enjoy the prestige passed down from his grandfather. People seek alliances with members of lineage with long established reputations rather than with those who have recently accumulated wealth and earned a reputation, since a person from a good lineage maintains the good name and prestige of the family.

THE KINDRED AND THE FAMILY

The kindred group or *kutumb* differs from the lineage in its structure as well as in its functions. The group is larger than a *parivar* (family) which is composed of a definable number of persons related through patrilineal ties. The *kutumb* is a broader term which embraces both the agnates and the cognates. The term *kutumb* tends to be understood as an extended composite family. The cooperation of its members is continually sought at ritual occasions, and their status is validated by the custom of the lineage. Though the views of the patrilineal kin predominate in all matters of family decisions, inheritance, business, marriage alliances, and ritual observances, due consideration is given to the views of the cognates.

The family is the patrilineal group composed of a unit or units of several households and does not include any matri-kin. While the members of this group share a common dwelling and cooking hearth, pool their incomes and property, spend jointly for all purposes, and perform rituals together, they continue to be one family. When they become independent, they may still be known as an extended family even though they no longer function as one.

Each person belongs to a lineage, clan, *parivar* (family), and subcaste or caste. The local lineage and the caste group are the effective operating units.

The commonly held belief is that the best kind of family is one in which two or more married men, usually related through close kin ties, live together with their married sons and their families, and sometimes with grandparents and unmarried daughters. Such a composite group is commended for its unity and considered prestigious. Such a family will continue to function as long as its physical resources permit it to. However, this type of family is becoming incapable of satisfying the ever-growing demands of the younger members. The pressures of family obligations have been lessened and a young person is not under the same obligation that his parents were. The large family is being destroyed by the desire of its younger members to migrate to urban areas for better occupations and to move up on the social scale through secular accomplishments of wealth and power.

Although a variety of marriage practices have been instituted by the different castes in Awan, each is generally suited to the needs of the caste in its particular situation. For example, polygamy and remarriage are much more prevalent among the lower castes. Since the lower castes generally consider women to be primarily a part of the labour force, the addition of extra women to a family is a commendable objective. Also, since the lower castes are generally attempting to improve their economic position, a second marriage which may be helpful in adding another contributor to the family economy as well as prestige to the man is looked upon favourably. However, though most of the remarriages lead to reorganisation of the family, yet polygynous marriages are considered a potent cause of family dissensions. The practical needs of the caste instil an appreciation for the caste marriage practices in the families of the caste, which in turn instils a respect for the practices in the children, perpetuating the practices. This does not mean that marriage practices of a caste may not change or that changes are not even encouraged, but any change which takes place must take place within the pragmatic framework of the needs of the caste members. A male child is necessary for the perpetuation of lineage and a family's name which is considered to be of paramount importance. At all levels of the social hierarchy the formal superiority of the male is recognised. Propitiatory rites for the family's ancestral spirits are particularly importance in the families of upper castes. Divergent views are held about fosterage and adoption among different castes, with the twice-born castes being more particular about the formal status of the adopted child. If a man and his wife are unable to procreate a male child, or no male child has survived, the couple would generally bring one into the family from the same clan group. However, occasionally people will choose one of their daughter's sons as the inheritor of their property. Fostering a child does not automatically lead to the transfer of property rights to the child. The transfer must be validated by formal injunction.

An adopting person follows certain criteria for choosing the boy he wishes to adopt. Usually his choices would run from the boy of his nearest agnatic group, to the composite family, then to the local and the dispersed lineage group, to the broader clan group, and ultimately to the whole subcaste or caste. Any member of the clan is customarily a prospective inheritor, but the adopting person has to formally declare one. Certain rites of inheritance are publicly performed, and for all legal purposes entries are made in documents.

Giving a child for adoption enables a poor man to increase his financial resources and place himself in better social circumstances. His son's newly achieved prestige and some of its benefits are transmitted to the members of his natal family also. A boy who has inherited the riches of someone would not command respect among the kinsmen and the villagers unless he has been well accepted by the adopting couple and the local people. In some cases the adopting couple and the parents of the child continue to examine the assets of such alignments for several years and make and unmake decisions to their advantage.

When a man's wife is unable to give birth to a male child the most commonly accepted practice is to marry another woman. Begetting a son is one of the crucial reasons for polygyny. However, it often leads to family quarrels and can become very expensive. A husband in such a family is usually unhappy because of the dissension among his wives and often sets up a separate household for the childless wife. It is uncommon for the upper castes to turn to polygyny in the absence of a male child, since the upper caste families are in a better position economically to attract a person for adoption and such a marriage hurts the prestige of the second bride's family. A polygynous family is no longer considered prestigious although it was in the feudal past. Another reason that polygyny is frowned upon is that additional women in the family among the agriculturists and artisans are economic assets. Since they are responsible for a great deal of work in the home and the fields, families are reluctant to give them up to a man who has one wife already.

In the whole process of adoption there is an overtone of superordinate-subordinate relationships. The adopting person is superior, usually relatively rich and transcendental in his approach, while the adopted person is inferior, usually poor and pragmatic in his ends.

It is also possible for a couple with daughters but no sons

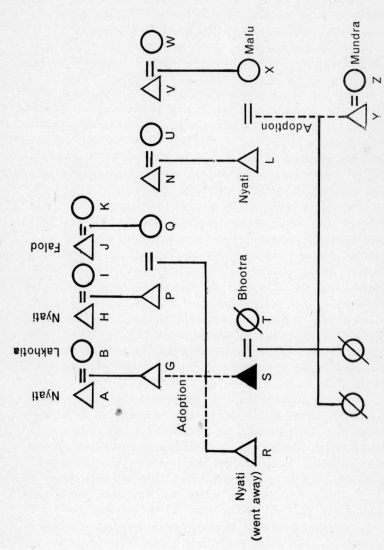

Fig. 2. Adoption of the male children and avoidance of clans for marriage alliances among the Maheshwari Mahajans.

to marry a daughter to a boy who would agree to live with his in-laws and help them with their farming ventures or business. One of the major faults of such adoptions is that they do not provide for the succession of the lineage. Also, this type of arrangement usually results in a poor marriage for a girl, since a man living with his in-laws is not in a prestigious position and the more socially desirable men are usually unwilling to do so. However, for the husband such a stigma is counterbalanced by the marital alliance, possibly with a superior girl, and the prestige gained by the riches he inherits (cf. Klass 1966: 1960; Madan 1965: 62, 127-128; Fututake, *et al.* 1964: 139). Such an arrangement is also advantageous to the in-laws since it provides someone to help them with the family affairs and to manage the transmittal of their estate to the children of their daughter. A son-in-law may satisfy one of the more important functions of a son by having male children who make up for the absence of male children in the family. In the end the parents are still able to pass their wealth down to children who have blood ties with them.

Two kinds of well-defined structural rules are followed in adoption: those suggesting whom to adopt and whom not to, and the implicit rules of the game of maneouvring for family advantage. We have discussed both sets of rules. To illustrate how these rules are observed to maintain the exogamous character of the family after adoption, a caste has been analysed.

On the occasion of the marriage of S (Figure 2) the clans of SQIK were avoided, because S was married before he was adopted. During Y's marriage, the clans of YXUW and T were avoided since T and X held a common status and after adoption T became Y's mother. Further avoidance ascending upon the generation of the adopting person was not followed. The avoidance of five clans in this manner was meant to avoid the probability of Y's marital alliance with a girl bearing the clans of his new mother T.

An examination of the avoidance patterns for the matrimonial alliances of the Maheshwari Mahajan reveals: (*i*) social relations dominate biological relations for establishing new kin ties; (*ii*) avoidance of clans of the adopting person and the adopted person encompasses a greater area of kinship to rule out the probabilities of incest and to facilitate a clear line of succession;

(*iii*) avoidance of the adopting person's wife's clan for the marital alliance of an adopted boy reiterates her recognition as mother and the position of her natal relatives with the adopted person and vice-versa; (*iv*) in other cases, generally the avoidance of the adopting person's wife's clan also emphasises her relations with the adopted son as a mother-son relationship and thereby eliminates chances of sexual relations with the adopting person's wife's sisters and daughters.

Fostering a male child for the purpose of adoption is common to all castes and the child is treated as the real son of the adopting person. Therefore, all prohibitions which are applicable to the real son are applied to the adopted son. Adoptions thus may follow any one of three patterns: (*i*) adopting a male child of the same clan; (*ii*) fostering or adopting a male child of the nearest kin belonging to some other clan (for example, a sister's or daughter's son), and (*iii*) adopting a son-in-law. All of them are liable to inherit the property of the adopting person, but the continuity of the lineage is perpetuated by the first alternative only.

FICTIVE KINSHIP

Beyond the membership of a family, lineage and clan there are relations of a person diffused over the members of the subcaste, caste and the village community. Every member of a subcaste is either an agnatic kin or a potential affinal or feminal kin. Yet there are people within the village community or elsewhere who may be referred to by kinship terms who are not actually related. A visitor, particularly from a different cultural group, might find such usages confusing, though the villager is well aware of this customary practice. It should be clear that such usages are restricted to classificatory kinship terms only—irrespective of caste lines. However, at a broader level, except for the terms used for spouses, other terms are commonly used. Respect for age and the opposite sex is another significant element in these usages. For example, a young Brahmin man is well aware that his relationship with an old man of the leather-working caste is not the same as with his grandfather but he would use that kinship term while addressing him. To call an elder, irrespective of caste, by his real name is considered disrespectful. Deferential treatment is thus extended beyond the sphere of demarcated relationship. Calling a person by the kinship term suited to his age and sex institutes a closer, more personal relationship with complete strangers. The use of these terms is a formal gesture intended to indicate mutual respect and can be helpful in obtaining favours and resolving conflicts.

The use of fictive kinship terms cuts across the territorial boundaries of the village and is commonly used when a person refers to his mother's or wife's village. Almost all the people from such villages are subsumed within the framework of this kinship terminology.

Ideally, a person who has a married daughter in another village will not eat or drink while visiting the daughter's conjugal village. Such a practice can be attributed to the impact of fictive kinship which places all villagers of the son-in-law's village in the affinal category, and others from her own village in the natal category.

A person without blood relatives finds that these fictive bonds, strengthened by a relationship of mutual benefit and goodwill, provide him with his greatest source of security and protection. A clear distinction is made between kin ties which have a potential to become actual (through new affinal ties or revalidation of loose agnatic ties) and those that are maintained irrespective of the caste lines. A person can be a potential actual kin only within the caste but a fictional kin inside or outside the caste.

Of course not all people have the same opportunity to establish fictive kinship relations, nor are all those relationships established for the same purposes. Often these relationships are entered into by persons hoping to use the new relationship to manipulate the other person for their personal gain.

In Awan there is no segregation among children on the basis of sex or other differences until they reach the age of six or seven.

The birth of a boy is celebrated much more elaborately than the birth of a girl for several reasons. After a person's death only a son is able to perform the rites which will salvage the person's soul. A son is needed to carry on the lineage of the father and may become a great economic asset to his family. On the other hand, the birth of a daughter, though of less social consequence, brings a great virtue to the parents who are able to offer her as a sacred gift on her marriage. The economic implications of a girl's marriage, however, are largely responsible for the favouring of boys. While a family must be strong financially to attract a suitable husband for the girl, a boy strengthens the family's productive capabilities by bringing in an additional person and a handsome dowry when he marries. A girl is a financial liability to her family because of the cost of her wedding and the accompanying dowry. Also, the constant reminder that some day she will go to her husband's home gives an inferior status to the girl.

Ideally, young children respect and obey their parents. A boy devotes himself to the welfare of his parents and avoids any behaviour which runs contrary to their will. A girl who models her actions after her mother receives a great deal of affection from both parents.

The child's role gradually crystallises as time passes. A boy is expected to be outgoing while the girl must learn to stay at home.

Although boys are supposedly free, the parents seem to dictate the child's wishes. Generally, deference to parents entails a restrained relationship. A gradual ransition from open, demonstrative affection to a more formal and less familiar relationship between father and son usually takes place. A son is closer to his mother and the ties between them change with a lesser pace. Their bond is pure, tender and perhaps supreme. The boy passively observes the roles played by his parents, brothers and sisters as the ideals of family life. A boy, therefore, seldom fails to comply with his parents' wishes and directions and is expected to follow his parents' decisions concerning his marriage, occupation and several other plans. When he does not comply with their views, it is important that he attempts to circumvent rather than oppose them.

The most important area in which a child's parents hold complete control over his life is in the selection of the child's spouse. Hindu marriage, according to the villagers, is a *sanskara* —the most significant event of a person's life. Marriage is one of the sixteen *sanskaras* or stages through which the individual enters *grahasthashram* or the stage of married life (Kane 1941: 194). The individual is thus placed at the pivotal point when the question of marriage is discussed.

To the villager the institution of marriage fulfils four functions. First, marriage is a religious performance without which the individual is incomplete. The institution of marriage is considered to be a part of a person's *dharma* (religious duty). The sacrifices offered to the gods and deities by unmarried persons are said to be incomplete because a man is only half in himself. He becomes complete only after he secures a wife (cf. Kane 1941: 428-29). Second, marriage implies children who will carry the name of the father and *vansha* and become future caste members. Third, children are also necessary to assure a happy after-life for the parents. A son is needed to perform the funeral rites for a man after his death. A son is also given the responsibility of performing the *pani-dena* rite (oblations to the dead) which propitiates the *pitras* (souls of the agnatic ascendants). A daughter will some day be offered as the greatest gift possible through the rite of *kanyadan*. If there are no children to perform these rites, it is believed that a person's soul will not be saved. The fourth function of marriage is to satisfy the sexual desires of the partners in a socially acceptable manner. Bachelorhood is frowned upon since it is believed that a bachelor will be driven to a sinful life to satisfy his physical drives (cf. Kapadia 1966: 167-69).

The father of an unwed pubescent girl considers her status a grave sin and a cause of tremendous anxiety since the sexual drives which are awakening in her may bring him dishonour. The continuing presence of an unwed girl might bring supernatural retribution to the family. This is true only to a much lesser degree for boys.

NEGOTIATING A MARITAL ALLIANCE

Exogamy and Endogamy

Certain rules which determine who is and who is not a prospective spouse are explicitly followed during marriage negotiations. The person must belong to the endogamous category (caste and subcaste), yet not to the exogamous category (clan). Each subcaste and caste determines these rules for itself and also outlines the degree of prohibitions (see Chapter 4). One's own clan, one's father's mother's clan, one's mother's clan and one's mother's mother's clan usually fall into the prohibited categories, and an alliance with a person from these clans is believed to be incestuous. However, there are tendencies to limit the restrictions to one's own clan, one's mother's clan and one's father's mother's clans.

The types of marriages which are tabooed fall into three categories: positional, referential, and historical. Referential taboos forbid marriage between people in common reference categories who are related through actual patrilineal ties—such as the people placed in a lineage. Because of positional taboos, two persons in certain kin positions, such as a man and his aunt or his cousin, are forbidden to marry. Historical taboos forbid marital alliances between members who claim to have descended from one or more mythical or historical ancestors. According to Sanskritic usages, all these relations are collectively known as *sapinda* relations.

Intermarriage among people of the same village, however, is not prohibited and is generally practised by all castes. While the merits and demerits of local endogamy are discussed and variations do exist from caste to caste, fundamentally the approach is quite similar throughout the region. One question raised is how, when all villagers call each other brothers and sisters and are reared in the same locality, could they marry each other? But obviously, the term "brother", which refers to friendly ties among people, has quite a different use in this context than when it is applied to members of the same family.

One of the merits of village endogamy is that it helps in promoting local caste solidarity. Everyone becomes related through multiple kinship ties which strengthen the caste.

There is a correlation between the economic level of a caste and its practice of village endogamy. Prosperous families of wealthier castes prefer to seek alliances with their equals. Wealth is a very important factor among the upper castes since it is believed a bride's family must be perpetual donors to the groom's family. Those families who cannot expect to receive a large dowry usually do not go far from the village while seeking alliances, since marrying in a distant village is quite costly to both families. Many wealthy families, however, are willing to search as far as they can to find more profitable matches for their sons and daughters. The practice of giving a bride-price also increases the attractiveness of village endogamy among the artisans, agriculturists and other lower castes because it keeps the wealth within the village families.

Another effect of village endogamy is to enlarge the local caste more rapidly and strengthen it socially. A large caste which practises local endogamy usually manages to become a well-organised unit with a powerful caste organisation and strictly enforced caste rules. A low caste especially needs this unity since it lacks wealth, education, and professional skill. The general trend has been for numerically preponderant castes, such as the Mali, Dhakar, Kachhi and Balai, to first integrate for corporate action through strong kinship ties at the local level and then attempt to mobilise at the regional level.

Intra-village marriages are favoured among all the artisan and agricultural castes because women are considered economic assets. A local alliance allows a young wife to occasionally help her natal family during an especially busy harvest season or in a crisis situation. Her husband can also be an immense help to his in-laws. Since pre-puberty marriages remain popular, it is often several years before a girl joins her husband permanently. A local marriage makes the transfer of a girl from her natal to her conjugal home easier since it can take place gradually. It can, however, also make it easier for a girl to run home after a quarrel with her husband. While a girl's parents do not usually encourage this, her going home can relieve the tension between the couple or their respective families. Also, the possibility of the girl's return to her original family becoming permanent may be enough to frighten an overly demanding husband or an oppressive mother-in-law into becoming more understanding.

Several valid arguments can be cited against local marriages, one of which is that two families who are already very familiar with each other may jeopardise their relationship by entering into something as trying as marriage negotiations and an in-law relationship. Also, girls married locally are often charged with disloyalty to either family. Her loyalty to her husband's family is in continual conflict with her loyalty to her natal family. Often the conjugal family to whom the girl owes her primary loyalty becomes displeased when she continues to receive favours from her natal family. However, her natal family usually does not wish to annoy her new family since the girl will be living with them and in most cases the tensions which arise are gradually moderated by formal acknowledgement of ritual reciprocities between the two families. It is usually the girl's natal family, being in an inferior position, that takes the initiative in easing strained relationships.

The frequency of contact between the two families and its consequent impact is greatly increased if a person marries locally. The patri-families of Awan maintain that agnatic fraternal solidarity is much more important to them than feminal-affinal loyalty. It is a common saying that women are the cause of all family disruptions. Actually one of the factors responsible for such a charge is the practice of living in a common home and sharing duties and responsibilities related to rearing children and other household tasks. Under such conditions a woman's interests and the interests of her nuclear family are at times in conflict with the interests of the larger household. Also, the possibility of disagreements arising between her natal and conjugal kinsmen remains an ever-present hazard. It is for these reasons that local marriages are discouraged by many. Often the limited number of local caste members make a local marriage impossible, but when a family can afford it and their daughter is mature to handle the basic responsibility of domestic life, a marriage outside the village is preferred by many.

Another important reason people seek to marry their children outside the village is to enlarge their circle of connections within the caste. For a person with economic or political ambitions that extend beyond the village locality and local caste organisation, a marital alliance outside the village would be a valuable bond, since kinship ties hold considerable weight. A good marriage outside the village also adds to an individual's prestige.

While a caste which is promoting local marriages may be a locally powerful unit, it is weak outside the village and less vulnerable to the external forces of change. However, an individual's innovativeness and a caste's ability to adapt itself to progress are hindered to a much lesser degree by a small local caste unit than a large one.

FORMAL HIERARCHY AND FLEXIBILITY IN MARRIAGE NEGOTIATIONS

Although local customs dictate that it is the responsibility of a girl's father to find her a suitable mate, it is only among a few upper castes (Brahmin, Rajput, Mahajan and Kayastha) that negotiations are made by a girl's representative. In all the agricultural and artisan castes the boy's family usually initiates the action. This practice illustrates the attitude of the upper caste which hold the status of the girl's family much lower than that of the boy's family. As such, most of the lower castes have begun to claim that in their caste the girl's family initiates a marriage proposal. While diplomacy prevents the boy's family from formally recognising the inferiority of the girl's family while assessing the status of her family, this consideration is inherent in the process. Even if the two families are of about the same status, they naturally compete to gain every advantage possible in the negotiations. Ideally, two families of equal status will more easily form a peaceful alliance.

ASTROLOGY

Many factors are taken into consideration before initiating a marriage proposal in the local community and surrounding villages and towns. These considerations include the day and time of the venture as well as the direction in which the person must travel. The priest is usually asked to determine the most appropriate day for the journey. The various supernatural forces which may affect the course of the couple's married life are also considered. All omens are carefully observed since any negligence might later cause misery. Although astrological phenomena are not clear to every individual, it is believed that the success of a marriage is highly dependent upon the congruence of the horoscopes of the prospective couple. Horoscopes are believed to be the principal link between a person and the cosmic world. Most village priests are able to devise reliable moment by moment schedules of an individual's life cycle, which is presumably determined at the time of his birth.

The fortune of a person is thought to move in accordance with the cosmic world. Similar horoscopes indicate that two people will be compatible as spouses. Some go as far as saying that two people are predestined to marry. This kind of belief usually pre-empts a high degree of rationalisation in marriage negotiations.

People are also able to find ways to manipulate astrology for their own benefit and often find it a convenient way to rationalise their personal shortcomings. Such things as an unsuccessful marriage or a poor business transaction are often blamed on a person's horoscope. It is always possible for the people who practise the art to re-examine the horoscopes and arrive at completely different conclusions. A brief rite might be all that is needed to change a sign from unfavourable to favourable. On the other hand, a negative astrological calculation is a very good excuse for tactfully withdrawing a proposal. If a person decides not to accept a proposal, it is always possible to find an astrologer who will create an insurmountable barrier to that particular match.

The basic unit of astrological calculations used in determining compatibility of a prospective couple is known as *biswa*. Usually 15 to 25 units of agreeement would make a very good match. However, there are other details which must be observed. For example, a subject who bears a *mangal* celestial name should marry someone with the same type name, or else risk the possibility of encountering serious crises. Still, marriages which contradict these principles do occur, and whenever a suitable match is not available, all these rules are superseded by special blessings of the gods and deities. Occasionally, a premature death of either spouse is blamed on an incongruence in their astrological attributes. While such beliefs express a complex view of man and his society in which institutional norms connect him with the cosmic world, these beliefs also suggest that man's fate and his role in society is predestined and largely irrevocable and immutable.

RITES OF BETROTHAL

As soon as two families decide that their children are to be married, the prospective bride and groom take part in certain rites and ceremonies. To insure formal social acceptance of the marriage, the *tilak* rite is performed, which indicates the boy has been chosen by the girl's family. While the *tilak* rite is not a legal contract, its breaches are met by severe public criticism. It is before the *tilak* that both the families must agree what benefits each will receive from the marriage. The *tilak* rite is performed by a representative of the girl's family at the house of the prospective bridegroom. Such things as clothing, small jewelry and cash are offered to the young man by the girl's representative. Among castes in which girls are scarce, such ceremonies tend to be simple and inexpensive. However, where boys are scarce even a family of modest means can expect to receive extravagant gifts. Such processes mark several kinds of transactions between the families until the couple are married.

The *tilak* rite is considered more binding by some than it is by others. For example, it is not uncommon for Brahmins to honour a *tilak* even after being tempted by much more lucrative offers. The Rajput also take pride in the honour they bestow upon the *tilak* rite.

However, it is always possible that a more attractive offer could lead to the dissolution of the earlier one. The health, apperance, level of education, and family wealth of a new suitor could break an engagement in the same way as those factors were instrumental in bringing about the engagement in the first place.

Sagai

The next step in strengthening the initial alliance is performance of a rite known as *sagai*. Usually, this rite follows the *tilak* ceremony and precedes the wedding. Again, on this occasion a representative of the girl's family visits the family of the boy and ceremonially offers gifts to him and to his parents. Members of the caste, friends and relatives are invited to witness the *sagai* ceremony. The quality of the gifts, the money offered to the boy's family and the presence of important members of the community indicate the prestige of the family. It is a common belief that the success of the *sagai* feast will forecast the quality of the wedding.

The process of marrying a child is very competitive. There are those who suffer from the stigma of breaking an alliance and those who gain prestige by obtaining a better one. It is a complex game in which each family attempts to gain as much as possible from the other family and at the same time give as little as it can. There is also the continual threat that any agreement which they may reach may be broken if the other family receives a more attractive offer before the marriage. Customarily, the girl's family is expected to appease the boy's family continually with gifts on festive occasions.

Breaches of *sagai*, which are uncommon, occur most frequently in cases where either family suddenly finds itself in a better bargaining position. It is considered more serious when a boy's family breaks an engagement; then the girl and her family suffer a great loss of prestige. Once a poor reputation is earned, people begin to question the integrity of the girl and her natal family and it may become difficult to find a suitable match for her. While both families lose a certain amount of respect, the girl's family's reputation always receives the most serious injury. They also lose financially, since up to the wedding they must give nearly all the gifts. In the village and its surrounding region a family is ranked by its caste; within the caste a family's wealth and prestige determine its social position. The drive for social gains continues to motivate people to compete for every possible prize, including marriage partners.

The village *gaonguru* (the priest who belongs to the Sandhaya Brahmin caste) is consulted for a *muhurt* (the time at which the rite should be performed). After consulting an almanac he suggests several favourable times. If no one point can be fixed the next choice can be a sacred day, or in certain cases the *sagai* proposal is consecrated at the feet of the Ganesh deity. The *gaonguru*, the family Nai and the drummer are sent for and the Nai is sent to invite all the neighbours and caste members to attend the ceremony.

The boy is asked to sit on a wooden plank in the presence of the guests. The plank is placed on a design prepared with wheat flour, turmeric powder and rice. Barley and maize are used to support the *kalasha*—a brass bowl of water covered with red cloth. A few plates containing the articles sent by the bride's party are also arranged around the bridegroom. The representative of the bride's party stands up and puts a *roli* mark on the forehead of the prospective bridegroom and then presses a few grains of rice into the *roli*. Then the bride's representative places a *pagdi* or *safa* (turban) on the boy's head. During this ceremony the priest recites the *mantras* and a set of clothes, some cash, dry fruits and articles such as a gold chain or a wrist watch are put in the boy's lap. Then the boy's father is presented with a head dress, a set of clothes, and a rupee. The priest fastens *lacchas* (multicoloured threads) on the right hand of the boy, his father's and the bride's representative. The bride's representative places a *roli* mark on the forehead of the priest, offers him a rupee, and drops a rupee in the plate containing the articles of worship. The Nai and the drummer are also awarded Re 1 each. The Nai receives a turban and an *angocha* (napkin) for his services. He then washes the plate and the drummer beats his drum awhile. The boy's brother-in-law gives a handful of *gur* or *patasha* (solidified sugar sweets) to everyone assembled for the occasion.

The performance of these rituals may vary widely, as can be seen from several examples which took place in Awan. During the *sagai* of Krishna, a Brahmin trader 19 years old, the village priest Ram Gopal was called. Of the thirty persons assembled, only four belonged to his own caste. The uncle of the girl brought the material for the ceremony of *sagai*. The family Nai's wife plastered the floor with clay and cow-dung, and decorated it with white designs. She also fastened a *bandarwal* (mango twigs reinforced with jute strings) above the door as a symbol of the occasion The women from the neighbouring families sang songs to propitiate the gods and deities, repeating verses to insert the names of all adult male members of the family. At the end of the ceremony 50 gms. of *gur* was given to each individual at the ceremony.

The priest was given Rs 4 as *dakshina*, the Nai Rs 1.40 and a turban, his wife a scarf and two kilograms of wheat, and the drummer Re 1 and one kilogram of wheat.

The entire Mali caste was invited to the *sagai* of Nanda, a 15 year old Mali boy with elementary education. The girl's brother brought the *sagai* gifts. The priest declared a *muhurt* of 3 p.m. Thirty-one women and ten men witnessed the *sagai* ceremony from the *chabutaras* of the house. It was accompanied by women singing and dancing. In the evening several young men formed a separate group and participated in the dances. Liquor was served and the *sagai* celebrations continued until late that night. The Nai and the drummer were given Rs 3 and Re 1 respectively, along with a few grams of corn. The Kumhar, Kalal, Khatik, Luhar, Dhobi, Balai, Mer, Bola and Harijan are the only castes which serve liquor on such occasions.

Ghisia Balai had an offer for the *sagai* of his son Prema from a village located twenty-one miles away. He went to the village with his son for a *baithba* (a visit to console a mourning family). The *panchas* of the caste insisted that he accept a marriage proposal for his son and he readily agreed. A simple *tilak* ceremony was performed by the girl's father who presented Prema with Re 1, one coconut and 500 gms. of sweets. The event was so arranged that no rituals were observed before the marriage. It was estimated that Rs 650 was spent during the marriage.

Mohan, a twenty-year-old Bhangi was married to a girl from the village of Khera, located five miles away. The *sagai* proposal was initiated by the girl's father six months before the marriage. The girl's father requested Mohan to accept the proposal and make a cash payment of Rs 300 as dowry. Since Mohan's father was no longer living, he said he would be able to pay only half that price. The father of the girl accepted and was entertained for two days before returning to his village.

Two months later the marriage took place. Mohan's *sagai* ritual consisted merely of his receiving the *roli* mark on his forehead and being offered a coconut by his prospective father-in-law. *Tilak* and *sagai* are usually observed as two distinct rituals by the upper castes but occasionally are combined in special cases when the wedding must take place immediately. Among the agricultural and lower castes these two rituals tend to take place on the same occasion. With the exception of a few educated families, the Kachhi and Mali perform both rituals together, while the Darjee, the Sunar, the Tamboli and the Teli observe *tilak* and *sagai* separately.

AGE AT MARRIAGE

It is a common practice for girls to marry before reaching puberty. There are several arguments advanced in favour of early marriage. The people believe early marriages tend to protect the chastity of women, ease the transfer of a girl from her father's domain to that of her husband, and make it easier for a girl to adjust to her husband and in-laws. Pre-puberty marriages are also considered to be more sacred and pure than a marriage which takes place later in a girl's life, since the girl has not been contaminated by the pollution associated with menstruation. It is also feared that a girl's approaching sexuality will lead her to relinquish her sacred status as a virgin. It is well known that the Sanskritic scriptures of the Vedic times state that a girl should be married as a virgin and before menarche.

The economic consideration is also very important. A girl married before puberty becomes an economic partner in her conjugal family much earlier. This, in turn, reintegrates the economy of her natal as well as conjugal family.

Traditionally, each incipient family begins with the support of an old family. The young people are responsible for bringing new people into the family, both by marriage and by birth, to replace the old members. Since marriages are expensive events, the family's economy must be preserved by spacing marriages several years apart. The earlier the marriage is organised, the better it is for the family. Parents like to see their responsibilities fulfilled before they retire. Most marriages cost somewhat more than a year's income of the family. In some cases, as among the Rajputs, a marriage may take two to three year's of the family's income. Early marriages of the children help the family to space the marriages evenly.

Another advantage of early marriages is that a person benefits immediately from any advantages he has achieved through the marital alliance.

However, on an average the boys are usually married between the age of 12 to 16 years, while the girls are married between the age of 9 and 14 years. Analysing the caste rank and its relationship with age at marriage, it appears that there is little association between the two. One of the major inferences could be that it is not the rank of the caste, but its involvement in agricultural activities which could explain the distribution of age at *sagai* and marriage. For purposes of broader generalisation three perceivable trends can be delineated: (*i*) upper castes marry relatively late, (*ii*) agriculturists and artisans marry relatively early, and (*ii*) most of the boys and girls among all the castes continue to marry earlier than the minimum aged fixed by the Hindu Marriage Act of 1955, which is 15 for girls and 18 for boys. Obviously, the legislation relating to the age at marriage has had little impact, if any, on the marital practices of the people.

The above analysis also suggests that age at marriage in itself cannot be an objective index depicting the virtual transfer of a girl from her natal family to conjugal family. It was noticed that actual living of the girl in her conjugal family varied from six months to six years, which was generally dependent on her education, age at marriage, size, occupation, economy and locality of natal and conjugal family.

SOCIAL AND RESIDENTIAL PROPINQUITY

The marital alliances are a manifestation of the diffusion of effective kinship ties of castes distributed over a region. Leaving aside the variables of concentration of a caste in a particular sector of the cultural region and the preferences for making choice for mate selection, the data available substantially support a positive correlation between economic and propinquity variables in marriage patterns. In-village marriages within the limits of the *gotra*-avoidance rules are permitted among all the castes of the village. Obviously, the larger and more highly differentiated the population of a caste group in the village the fairer the chances of in-village marriages.

Often a small caste population comprises a small number of families, usually related through agnatic ties and often split into factions due to professional competition. An analysis of 321 marriages reveals that during 1935-65, out of 19 castes, 11 have contracted marriages within the village. Also, nearly 20 per cent (62) of the marriages have occurred between the residents

Table 2

MEAN AGES AT SAGAI AND MARRIAGE OF BOYS AND GIRLS AMONG
THE MAJOR CASTES FROM 1935 TO 1965

Caste	*No. of families*	Boys			Girls		
		No. of marriages	*Age at sagai*	*Age at marriage*	*No. of marriages*	*Age at sagai*	*Age at marriage*
Brahmin	44	19	14	16	21	9	12
Rajput	16	10	15	16	9	10	13
Mahajan	15	8	16	17	12	12	14
Ahir	7	4	14	16	4	9	11
Dhakar	43	15	12	14	16	8	10
Mali	53	14	10	13	15	8	12
Kachhi	145	29	8	12	32	12	9
Khati	5	3	14	16	4	12	14
Luhar	6	3	11	14	2	10	13
Kumhar	8	5	12	14	3	8	10
Teli	7	4	13	14	5	11	12
Nai	5	4	12	16	3	9	13
Dhobi	6	3	9	13	4	7	12
Mogya	5	1	10	13	2	12	13
Khatik	16	11	11	14	9	8	10
Balai	52	14	12	15	11	9	11
Mer	9	5	11	15	7	8	11
Bola	5	1	12	14	1	8	12
Bhangi	5	5	10	13	3	8	10
Total	452	158	12	15	163	9	12

of the village. In the case of 259 out-village marriages, as many as
13 castes have sought alliances no further than 25 miles from the
village, 4 went no further than 15 miles, and two went no further
than 45 miles (cf. Cohn and Marriott 1958; Gould 1960: 486;
Marriott 1955, 176; Mayer 1960: 208, 299).

Few marriages occur beyond the radius of 100 miles, though in a very few cases higher castes have gone as far as 400 miles to make matches even though they have been quite populous in the surrounding area.

Table 3 suggests that at least four generalisations could be derived on the basis of the analysis of 321 marriages. (*i*) The higher castes, on an average, tend to make marital alliances in relatively distant villages and towns. Spearman rank order correlation between caste rank and average distance in miles was computed, which is 0.65 and is also significant beyond .01 level. (*ii*) Those castes that give expensive dowries, particularly the Brahmin, Rajput, and Mahajan, necessarily spend more on marriage of girls. Therefore, those castes who are economically well-off, and those who emulate the wedding patterns of these twice-born have a tendency to go much farther to seek marital alliances. (*iii*) Better economic resources of a caste contribute to higher age at marriage along with chances of seeking marital alliances from a wider area. Similarity of socio-economic status is believed to be one of the major axes for binding people into marital alliances within a caste. Therefore, a highly differentiated caste is more likely to explore and establish marital ties over a broader region; and (*iv*) economically well placed castes, able to incur heavier expenditures on marriages, are able to attract mates and invite friends to marriages from distant places, thereby promoting newer ties over a broader region.

EDUCATION

The educational ambitions which parents instil in their children are determined by the occupational affiliation of the family, the economic resources available and the parents' attitude toward formal education. Instilling these ambitions may be regarded as a two-step process. The socio-economic status of the parents and the ambitions associated with that status govern the type of socialisation process that the children will be put through. This process in turn instils parental ambitions into the children. According to this reasoning, any change in the world view and circumstances of parents would change the future ambitions of their children and provide children with culturally enriching activities and pressure them to excel in those fields which may be greatly rewarding. This discussion takes into account whether

Table 3

CASES OF MARRIAGES IN AND OUTSIDE THE VILLAGE AMONG
THE MAJOR CASTES

Caste	No. of families	No. of marriages	Marriages within the village	Marriages outside the village	Maximum distance in miles	Average distance in miles
Brahmin	44	40	3	37	300	36
Rajput	16	19	3	16	152	43
Mahajan	15	20	—	20	400	23
Ahir	7	8	—	8	85	24
Dhakar	43	31	13	18	85	19
Mali	53	29	7	22	65	20
Kachhi	145	61	23	38	58	21
Khati	5	7	—	7	105	23
Luhar	6	5	1	4	46	14
Kumhar	8	8	1	7	52	26
Teli	7	9	—	9	63	19
Nai	5	7	—	7	52	35
Dhobi	6	7	1	6	45	31
Mogya	5	3	—	3	15	15
Khatik	16	20	5	15	60	18
Balai	52	25	4	21	48	15
Mer	9	12	1	11	51	19
Bola	5	2	—	2	26	13
Bhangi	5	8	—	8	16	12
Total	452	321	62	259		

early marriages contribute positively or negatively to the educational achievements of the subjects, and also stresses that a positive correlation exists between the three variables of economic resources, educational attainments and the age at marriage. Analysis of the data from the village school, which attracts students from 13 other villages, reveals that out of 348 students, 98 (28 per cent)

Table 4

MARITAL STATUS OF THE STUDENTS OF THE HIGHER SECONDARY SCHOOL IN AWAN IN 1965*

Class or Grade	Students			Married Students				Year		
	Male	Female	Total	Male	Female	Total	% of Total	Average age at sagai	Average age at marriage	Inter-vening period
V	46	6	52	6	—	6	11.5	10.5	12.0	1.5
VI	69	6	75	14	—	14	18.6	11.5	13.0	1.5
VII	41	2	43	9	—	9	20.9	12.0	14.0	2.0
VIII	38	—	38	13	—	13	34.2	13.0	15.5	2.5
IX	48	—	48	10	—	10	20.8	14.5	16.5	2.0
X	42	2	44	15	2	17	38.6	15.5	17.5	2.0
XI	48	—	48	29	—	29	60.4	16.0	18.0	2.0
	332	16	348	96	2	98	28.1	13.3	15.2	2.0

*Out of the 348 students enrolled in the school, 198 came from other neighbouring villages. The author is grateful to the Head Master of the local Higher Secondary school for his help in obtaining information from the students and the school records.

Table 5

DISTRIBUTION OF STUDENTS ACCORDING TO CASTE, EDUCATIONAL LEVEL AND MARITAL STATUS IN 1965*

Castes	Class or Grade							Total	% Married
	V	VI	VII	VIII	IX	X	XI		
Twice-born castes:									
1. Brahmin	9	12	6	5(1)	9(1)	18(3)	16(7)	75(12)	⎫
2. Rajput	2	3	4	1(1)	2	1(1)	—	13(2)	⎬ 13.3
3. Mahajan	4	5	7	8	12	14(2)	12(4)	62(6)	⎭
Non-twice-born castes:									
4. Agriculturists: Ahir Dhakar, Gujar, Kachhi, Mali, etc.	18(3)	21(8)	9(4)	8(5)	6(5)	4(4)	11(9)	77(83)	⎫
5. Clean artisans: Khati, Luhar, Kumhar, Teli, Nai, etc.	13(2)	22(3)	14(2)	11(1)	17(4)	6(6)	9(9)	92(27)	⎬ 39.4
6. Unclean artisans: Dhobi, Mogya, Khatik, Balai, Mer, Bola, etc.	6(1)	11(3)	3(3)	5(5)	2	1(1)	—	28(13)	⎭
7. Untouchables: Bhangi	—	1	—	—	—	1(1)	—	1	
Total	52(6)	75(14)	43(9)	38(13)	48(10)	44(17)	48(29)	348(143)	

*The data were obtained from the village Higher Secondary school and from the students in the summer of 1965. The student population under study includes those students who come from eleven other villages of the surrounding region.

Note: The number in parenthesis relates to married persons.

marry before they complete higher secondary education. The gradual growth in the number of married students from fifth through the eleventh standard (grade) obviously suggests that a large number of students (65 per cent) get married before they complete their education. Moreover, a substantial correlation exists between higher age at marriage and educational achievements. The time gap between betrothal and wedding has been extended for students who have gone for high school education. In brief, educational facilities have definitely influenced the world view of the people which, consequently, has resulted in better educational goals and higher age at marriage. This finding simply indicates that educational growth will most likely help in raising the age at marriage in general. The next question is: which people have benefited the most from the available resources?

Therefore, an examination of how economic dimension, predominated by caste rank, influences the marital patterns is desirable. Caste rank has a meaningful relation to the economic resources available to it, and, therefore, caste rank has often been subsumed under the rubric of "class."

Table 5 shows that higher castes, particularly the twice-born who are economically better off, do not marry their children early; only 13.3 per cent of the twice-born students were married as compared to 39.4 per cent among the non-twice-born students. In other words, the lower the rank of a caste, the higher the possibilities of early marriage, but the lesser the chances of parental persuasion for better educational plans. Chi-square test found the difference between the twice-born and the non-twice-born students significant beyond the .001 level with the twice-born students having lesser tendency of marrying at relatively lower age and before completing their high school or higher secondary education.

Data indicate that nearly 43 per cent of the students come from less than 20 per cent of the village population, while 57 per cent are from the non-twice-born castes which form more than 80 per cent of the village population.

Possibly the pressure used by the upper caste parents on their children to go to school is relatively more important and consistent with the caste rank and also with meeting the needs of their occupations, as compared with that used by agriculturist and artisan parents.

Education, though considered greatly rewarding and a significant means by which to move upward on the social scale, is not a major prerequisite for marriage in a large section of the lower caste population. Though a college education is believed to equip persons for better opportunities, it threatens the joint economy of the family. College education also gives an independent status to the individual who usually migrates to the town or city to improve his life chances. Early marriage serves as a deterrent to such enterprises as well as a stabilising force for traditional family unity.

A person who acquires an education often acquires with it a taste for some of the finer things which his village cannot provide. He is torn between the desire to learn the skills necessary to hold a well-paying position in the city and the desire to serve his family, caste, and native community. The compromise which is most often reached is that the person will live in the urban area while taking care of his parents and family in the village financially.

EXPENDITURE ON WEDDINGS

Though caste hierarchy in itself is not an objective measure for obtaining an understanding of the Indian stratification system, considerable consistency seems evident between caste and class stratifications in this region.

Table 6 indicates a high correlation between caste and class rank order. Spearman correlation was computed and found to be 0.75 which is significant beyond .01 level. The upper castes are placed high not only because they are ritually pure, but also because they are economically superior. It is interesting to note, however, that there are some families of artisans and agriculturists who are economically no better off than those of the sweepers, who are at the bottom of the ritual hierarchy.

A wedding carries immense importance socially and economically in the network of relationships. The family's wedding expenditure sets its position in the status scale. Those castes who are economically dominant had much to spare for wedding celebrations while those who were poor had exceedingly little to spare. The data suggest that a family spends between nine months to more than a year's income on a girl's wedding. The relatively high expenditure for a girl's marriage is the result of the practice

Table 6

DISTRIBUTION OF MAJOR CASTES ACCORDING TO ANNUAL INCOMES IN AWAN

S. No.	Caste	No. of families	Numbers of families with their annual incomes in rupees													Average income
			less than 500	501-1000	1001-1500	1501-2000	2001-2500	2501-3000	3001-3500	3501-4000	4001-4500	4501-5000	5001-5500	5501-6000	6001 & above	
1.	Brahmin	44	—	2	5	6	4	3	11	9	—	—	—	—	4	3,062
2.	Rajput	16	—	—	2	8	6	—	—	—	—	—	—	—	—	1,250
3.	Mahajan	15	—	—	3	—	—	2	1	2	—	—	—	—	7	4,400
4.	Ahir	7	—	2	2	2	—	1	—	—	—	—	—	—	—	1,465
5.	Dhakar	43	2	8	10	4	9	3	7	—	—	—	—	—	—	1,780
6.	Mali	53	3	10	26	6	3	1	4	—	—	—	—	—	—	1,350
7.	Kachhi	145	13	49	41	35	7	—	—	—	—	—	—	—	—	1,120
8.	Khati	5	—	—	—	2	2	—	1	—	—	—	—	—	—	2,340
9.	Luhar	6	—	1	3	2	—	—	—	—	—	—	—	—	—	1,850
10.	Kumhar	8	—	3	4	1	—	—	—	—	—	—	—	—	—	1,150
11.	Teli	7	—	1	2	2	—	—	—	—	—	—	—	—	—	1,585
12.	Nai	5	—	1	—	3	1	—	—	—	—	—	—	—	—	1,690
13.	Dhobi	6	—	3	3	2	—	—	—	—	—	—	—	—	—	1,160
14.	Mogya	5	1	3	1	—	—	—	—	—	—	—	—	—	—	800
15.	Khatik	16	—	6	4	2	2	—	2	—	—	—	—	—	—	1,100
16.	Balai	52	4	19	18	7	4	—	—	—	—	—	—	—	—	1,064
17.	Mer	9	—	6	2	1	—	—	—	—	—	—	—	—	—	940
18.	Bola	5	—	2	1	1	—	—	—	—	—	—	—	—	—	1,135
19.	Bhangi	5	—	5	—	—	—	—	—	—	—	—	—	—	—	954
	Total	452	23	119	127	84	41	10	26	11	—	—	—	—	11	

Note: The average income of the family is Rs 1509.

Table 7

AVERAGE EXPENDITURE ON MARRIAGES OF BOYS AND GIRLS ACCORDING TO CASTE

Caste	No. of families	Average income	Boys		Girls		Average difference in rupees
			No. of marriages	Average expenditure in rupees	No. of marriages	Average expenditure in rupees	
Brahmin	44	3,062	19	2,850	21	4,125	1,375
Rajput	16	1,250	10	2,720	9	5,200	2,480
Mahajan	15	4,400	8	3,920	12	6,750	2,830
Ahir	7	1,465	4	1,440	4	2,110	570
Dhakar	43	1,780	15	2,120	16	2,820	700
Mali	33	1,350	14	1,860	15	1,980	120
Kachhi	145	1,120	29	1,650	32	1,990	340
Khati	5	2,340	5	2,225	4	4,850	2,525
Luhar	6	1,850	3	1,680	2	2,730	1,150
Kumhar	8	1,150	5	1,340	3	2,600	1,260
Teli	7	1,585	4	2,450	5	3,010	560
Nai	5	1,690	4	2,230	3	3,110	880
Dhobi	6	1,160	3	2,380	4	2,540	160
Mogya	5	800	1	800	2	1,250	450
Khatik	16	1,100	11	1,980	9	2,630	650
Balai	52	1,064	14	1,620	11	1,988	268
Mer	9	940	5	1,200	7	1,290	90
Bola	5	1,135	1	1,250	1	1,300	50
Bhangi	5	954	5	650	3	860	210
Total	452		158		163		

of a bride's family bearing most of the wedding costs (cf. Epstein 1962: 342; Mayer 1960: 227).

Table 7 shows expenditure on the marriages of boys and girls by caste. Spearman rank order correlation coefficient between caste rank and average expenditure on marriages of both boys and girls is 0.99 which is significantly beyond .01 level. The pattern of expenditure suggests that as a family moves up on the economic scale it also has a greater chance of incurring greater expenses on weddings.

The economic differentiation between the twice-born and the non-twice-born castes is further displayed by the transferring of wealth through dowries from the bride's to the groom's family among the twice-born castes, which makes marriages immeasurably expensive. However, among the non-twice-born castes bride-wealth given by the groom's family lessens the economic burden on the bride's family even though dowries form a small part of the total expense of marriage. Large amounts are often borrowed from the family's landowner or from the caste council. Looking to the expenditure on girl's marriages it is common among non-twice-born caste for the amount of bride-wealth to be very close to the amount spent on dowry. However, the overall expenditure for a girl's marriage remains higher than for the marriage of a boy. Exceptions to these generalisations are based on personal features of the bride or groom such as personal charm, educational achievements, physical defects, and the expected success or failure of the person in his future endeavours.

Besides reinforcing and enlarging a family's network of relationships, weddings redistribute wealth, persons and resources. Dowries and bride-wealth can be understood as items which indicate both the social and ritual status of the caste. Once a lower caste family is able to improve its economic resources, it stops giving or receiving bride-wealth, an indicator of low status of a caste, and begins giving expensive dowries. This phenomenon may be observed in many of the marriages among the Khati, Luhar, and Kumhar.

A family's status and its chances for improving its status are determined by the cost of gifts exchanged among the kinsmen, caste fellows and friends, the obtaining of services from allies and artisans and the presence of the elite and political leaders.

Marriage remains a grand occasion to demonstrate a family's

prestige and a means to rise socially in the caste as well as through the whole social system. Depleting one's wealth by putting all one's resources into an expensive marriage is not uncommon. Although perpetual debts caused by these marriages sometimes jeopardise a family's esteem, public demonstration of a family's eminence is marked by the wealth it has been able to mobilise for such a pageant.

The formal beginning of the rites and ceremonies is the transition between a couple's engagement and their marriage. Typically, these rites and ceremonies portray the sacred unity of the couple and the status of the kinsmen, members of the caste, and friends. In addition to the cohesive role of the ritual acts performed together before the gods and deities, these also are planned to invoke divine and ancestral blessings. Some of these rituals help establish the beginning of a new relationship between the couple and their respective families. The core roles in the principal rituals are played by the bride and groom. Usually the roles of the kinsmen and friends are determined by the relationship each shares with the marrying couple and by the mutual courtesies extended in the past. Ritual performances clearly mark the hierarchy of the persons involved. Controversies about the ranking may lead to dissension, factional bickering and even to prolonged ill-feelings. However, a wedding is also the occasion for resolving such disputes and bringing about amicable settlements of old disagreements.

Weddings are the grand events in a family's life. The participation of the kinfolk and friends, receiving of gifts, and the formal celebration of the marriage rites illustrate the family's prestige and social position. All through the wedding the sacred prevails over the profane. The principal subjects and their respective families proclaim a span of divinity and provide an occasion for all kinds of aesthetic merriments. If there has been a death in the family, the pollution which the event is usually considered to inflict is nullified during this span. The houses are renovated, washed and decorated; musicians are called and the subjects are bedecked with jewels and costumes. The wedding provides a stage for a supreme pageant.

Lagan

A *lagan* is an auspicious complimentary letter sent by the girl's family inviting the bridegroom's party to solemnise the marriage on an appointed day. The letter, sprinkled with *kum-kum* and written in black ink, is wrapped with multicoloured thread. The Nai delivers the *lagan* and is provided with food, a garment and a rupee. The *lagan* in the bridegroom's family is placed at the feet of Ganesh and other gods. The acceptance of the *lagan* fixes the date of the marriage. Dishonouring the *lagan* hurts the prestige of the girl's family and is generally considered to be denying Lakshmi (the goddess of wealth) since she is personified by a lovely bride.

Bindyak-Baithana

Bindyak: When the *lagan* letter is received, it is opened before the *panchas* of the caste. The period between the opening of the *lagan* and the marriage ceremony may vary from a couple of days to a month, in accordance with the astronomical calculations. Before the marriage, the couple worships Ganesh and the deities of the family. The Brahmin priest officiates at the worship and the Nai arranges articles of worship in a metal plate. Women sing devotional songs.

The bride as well as the groom at their respective homes have a young boy who functions as an escort for each of them known as *bindyak*. He personifies the Ganesh deity, who is known as the remover of all obstacles, and continues to escort the bride or the groom until the wedding day.

The Painting of Ganesh Deity: As a token of reverence to the deity, a colour sketch of Ganesh with his maids Riddhi and Siddhi, sun and moon, *jwara* (green sprouts of corn), and his *vahan* the mouse is painted. This decorational work is generally performed by a professional painter of the Kumhar caste. He receives his *neg*, a ritual gift of cash ranging from 5 to 11 rupees, a head-dress and a coconut. On the occasion of the marriage, the walls of the house are whitewashed and decorated with paintings which include a variety of items such as gods, birds, monkeys, horses, camels, elephants, automobiles and trains, along with some sketches of domestic life. The elaborateness varies with the rank and the resources of the caste.

The Kum-Kum Patrika (wedding invitation): The text of the invitation card or the *kum-kum patrika* or *nyota* is prepared by an important person in the family and sent to a reputable printer. This card bears the miniature imprints of the Ganesh deity and his maids Riddhi and Siddhi on its upper side, and is flanked by *kalashas* containing flowers and buds. In the traditional script the first part of the card is devoted to invocation to all the gods and deities to grace the marriage with their presence. The second part is made up of the names of the male relatives of the bride or the bridegroom. The programme of major marriage rites is also listed. Mention is also made of the elderly members of the family on whose behalf the invitation has been extended. Among the agricultural caste groups and families of insufficient economic means, postcards are written in black ink and sprinkled with *kum-kum*. The Chamar and the Bhangi convey such information through the messengers of their own castes. Printed cards giving summarised information are now being increasingly used among the twice-born caste groups instead of elaborate letters.

The Bana and Ladian Songs (pre-nuptial songs): From the day of the *bindyak* ceremony, all rites begin with the singing of songs related to marriage and which invoke the deities. These songs are known as *bana* in the marriage of a boy and *ladian* in a girl's marriage. They usually depict the mythological events of marriage among the deities and are intended to invoke and propitiate the deities and the spirits of the ancestors of the family to bless the couple with a happy marital life. Certain rituals and events in the lives of past generations are described in the songs. They are sung during the days preceding the wedding by women who assemble each evening at the house of the bride or bridegroom. The women gossip and share reminiscences of their own marriages and those of their friends. After completing the series of songs, *patasha* gifts are given to each participant.

Binora (the pre-nuptial feast): Preceding the marriage, it is customary for the kinsmen, friends, and families of the caste to invite the bride or bridegroom to meals. This feast is known as *binora*. The strength of the friendship determines the number of persons invited. If the person hosting the *binora* is a very close friend, members of the extended kin group and neighbourhood may be asked to participate. These feasts are common to all castes but the quality of food differs noticeably from caste to caste. Participation in such feasts is governed by the rules of commensality. The lower castes exchange such feasts among themselves and such occasions are not many

Halad-hath and Snan (*Purificatory Rites*)

Halad-hath is a preparatory rite performed by five married women dressed in ritual robes and embellished with ornaments. The bride or groom sits on a wooden plank in the centre of the courtyard and is massaged with *haldi* (turmeric paste) by the Nai or his wife followed by a purificatory bath. The slab on which the paste is prepared is worshipped to pacify its anima. The paste is also presented to Ganesh and the deities of the family. Women gathered for the occasion sing devotional and marriage songs.

To invoke all the relevant gods and deities to help protect the marriage, married women assemble and go to the outskirts of the village headed by the drummer. There they collect a few stones to symbolise the deities and return singing devotional songs, "*Aāj Gajānand āvegā mhāri sabhā me rang barsāvegā...*" and "*Mātāne bhanwar ghadaun...*" to invite the benevolent gods and goddesses. These stone deities are placed in the company of Ganesh.

Tel-Chadhana (*Purificatory and Prohibitory Ritual*)

The purificatory and prohibitory ritual, *tel-chadhana*, is observed 5 to 7 days before the main wedding ceremony. The number of earthen pots for raising *jwar* (millet sprouts) and the number of women participants is determined by the number of days falling between the *tel-chadhana* and the actual day of the wedding.

The bride or groom is seated on a wooden plank, placed over a decorative design known as *chowk*. The women assembled for the ceremony sing devotional songs. Oil, *kum-kum*, *lachha* (multicoloured thread) are taken into *dauna* (leaf-cups). Each woman participant holds a *dauna* in her hands and touches it to the feet of the subject and then to the head. This process is repeated in accordance with the number of days intervening between *tel-chadhana* and the day of the wedding.

Kankan-dora Bhandhana (*Tying of the Marriage String*

For the ritual of *tel-chadhana*, a cotton thread fastened with a

lac and an iron ring and some *jwar* (millet) coloured with turmeric
is tied around the wiist of the right hand of the bridegroom and
on the left hand of the bride. This amulet is known as *kankan-
dora* (the marriage string). It is assumed that the amulet is animat-
ed with the powers which safeguard the subject from becoming a
prey for malevolent spirits. As such the subject is prohibited
from visiting spots suspected of being the abodes of malevolent
powers.

For their participation each of the women receives *neg* (ritual
gift) in cash or kind varying from one to five rupees each or an
article of equal value. The sister of the bride or groom performs
arti (waving of lights as a mark of adoration) before the subject.
She receives her *neg* from a quarter to two rupees among the agricultural and artisan castes and two to five rupees among the twice-
born caste groups. Devotional and marriage songs are sung
by the women at the end of the rite. The drummer beats the drum
at the entrance of the house during the ceremony.

Tai

Tai refers to the distribution of *gur* (molasses) among the
families of *vyayavaris*. This again indicates a scale of the type of
relationships maintained within the caste as well as the other
castes. *Paav* or quarter of a kilogram relates to a relationship of
a single degree and it may be multiplied up to four times the
number of persons to be invited to *binora*. The presents or clothes
and cash offered to the bride or the bridegroom's family are determined by the quantity of *gur* distributed among the families of
the caste and neighbourhood. The Nai of the family goes to
distribute *tai*. He is accompanied by a married woman who
represents the family.

Khanagar

Fresh clay is gathered for the wedding at a ceremony called
khanagar. The Nai's wife announces the beginning of the
khanagar ceremony to the members of the caste and neighbourhood. The assembled women form a procession with baskets and
axes in their hands. The procession is headed by a drummer and
the women sing devotional and marriage songs. The underlying
assumption is that fresh clay has to be brought for purificatory
rites to plaster the floor of the house.

Chari-Jhakolana (*Securing and Distributing Holy Water*)

Kalashas are the holy vessels of brass and copper covered with coloured cloth and flowers. Well water symbolically represents the holiest and the purest water—*Gangajal* (the water of the Ganges). The women go to a well known as *Amla* on the western side of the village and fill their *kalashas* or *gangajalis*. With the exception of the twice-born castes, earthen churns and bowls for *gangajalis* are used. Only the main pot used is made of brass. The women adorn themselves with new colourful dresses and ornaments and move in a procession headed by a musical band or a drummer. Some of the women bearing the *kalashas* nod their heads frequently, signifying their possession by the spirit of *Ganga*, the holy river goddess. The *kalashas* are preferably borne by 7 to 10 consanguine relatives. They are offered *patasha* or *gur*. The women unload the *kalashas* at the entrance of the house of the bride or bridegroom. The *neg* they receive ranges from 25 paise to Re 1. The water of these *kalashas* is taken out after a simple worship on the day of the *manda* feast. Each guest receives a few drops of the holy water. Widows and menstruating women are prohibited from participating in the ceremony.

Basan-Lana (*Bringing Earthen Churns to the Mandap Booth*)

Prior to the erection of the marriage booth and the main feast of *manda*, the *basan-lana* rite is observed. A group of ladies headed by the drummer go to the house of a potter to secure 5 to 7 *basan* (earthen churns). A few small bowls are also brought, in which *jwar* (millet) is raised. The women worship the potter's wheel and a plate of *seedha* (raw food material) is given to the potter. When the procession returns, the earthen pots are received by the father's sister's husband or sister's husband of the subject. He is given a *neg* ranging from rupee 1 to Rs 5, and the pots are placed in the cell of Ganesh deity. Some of them are arranged vertically along with the four poles of the *mandap* booth.

Binora

During the festive days of marriage, ceremonial processions are arranged for the bride and bridegroom. People such as sisters or close relatives meet the expenses of a musical band, drummer, fire-works, lampbearers, horseman, and *gur* or *patasha* distributed among the men and women who participate in the procession.

The procession is headed by the musical band or the drummer or both. The bridegroom or the bride riding on horseback is followed by the women who sing marriage songs. According to custom, the bride rides a stallion while the groom rides a mare. On the return the *arti* is performed by the sister or father's sister at the entrance of the house and she receives a *neg* of Re 1.

Manda-Garana

A *mandap* (a leafy canopy usually 6 to 8 feet in height) is erected in the courtyard of the bride's house. It is supported by four wooden rods. The holes for the erection of the poles are dug by the bride's uncle and the poles are erected by the Nai. Both receive *neg* ranging from Re 1 to Rs 5 and 25 paise to Re 1 respectively. The booth is adorned with green mango twigs, coloured paper and cloth stripes. Beneath this canopy, a *manda* or wooden rod 3 to 4 feet in height is erected with two cross-strips at the top and inverted small earthen saucers are suspended at the tips of the strips. The head of the family worships the *manda* before it is erected and the carpenter is paid Re 1 to Rs 25 in *neg*. Most important rites connected with the wedding are performed by the bridal couple under this canopy. A plough is placed in the groom's courtyard. The forms of the *manda* become symbols of the person's sex.

Mandal

The *mandal*, a ceremony to propitiate the gods and deities, is performed by the parents and closest agnatic kinsmen of the bride and the groom at their respective homes. In the absence of the senior agnatic couples cognatic couples may officiate. A purificatory *homa* is performed by the chief participating couple. The Brahmin priest officiates and chants *mantras* indicating the significance of the ceremony.

Manda-ki-Rasoi (*manda* feast): On the day of the ceremony, the *manda* feast takes place in the evening. In a boy's marriage it is organised before the groom's party departs for the home of the bride, and is the largest and the last in the sequence of marriage feasts, but in a girl's marriage it precedes one of the biggest feasts known as *goran*.

Passi: At the *manda* the members of the caste, neighbourhood, and friends offer *passi*, a cash gift along with a coconut, to the subject's family. The amount varies from 25 paise to Rs 2, depending on the nature of the relationship. *Passi* may be offered by a member of any caste. Even a Bhangi and a Chamar may offer *passi* to a Brahmin family, but the *passi* gifts are mutually exchanged among the first seven divisions only.

Pahravani

Pahravani refers to the ceremonial presentation of gifts to the couple who have performed *mandal-baithana* ceremony. The kinsmen and friends of the bride or groom offer a few *saropavas* (sets of dresses). However, the major brunt is usually borne by the person's maternal uncles and their families. The subject's mother's natal family pools resources and money to partially bear the expenses incurred during the marriage. Responsibility to act as the family's representative is usually assigned to one of the subject's senior or most suitable maternal uncles who offer a few sets of dresses, possibly with some jewellery and cash which form the *mausala*. The marriage of a sister's son is again an occasion to demonstrate brother's love by supporting his sister and her children. The cultural pattern demands continued favour and personal sacrifice on the part of the brothers to willingly help their sisters whenever an imbalance is caused in the family economy, such as by weddings. The *mausala* presents further become a means to strengthen ties and a measure of cordial and intimate relations between brothers and sisters (see Dube 1955a: 157-159; Dumont 1957: 36, 1961: 86-87; Madan 1965:213-215; Mayer 1960: 223-224). Friends and other kinsmen also offer some gifts of cash and dresses. After the ceremony the clothing is again given to the guests who had returned the gifts during the ceremony.

Nikashi

Savari: Nikashi is the procession of the bridegroom and his party to the bride's village. A mare is decorated with silver and gold polished ornaments for the *savari* (ceremonial ride). Colourful designs are embroidered on the saddle. For the initiation of the ceremonial ride the sister's husband performs the duties of the groom. He receives a *neg* ranging from Re 1 to Rs 5. The bridegroom is adorned in crimson bridal apparel along with necklaces of gold and garlands of flowers. The headdress, *safa* or *pagadi*, is embellished with golden ornaments such as *surpach*, *kilangi* and *turra*. A new pair of socks and shoes are worn by the bridegroom. A sword is also fastened at the waist with a *kamarbandh* (a six-foot-long crimson cloth). Among the twice-born caste groups a small *katar* (knife) is kept instead of the sword. Among the agricultural and lower castes silver ornaments are predominant, and the colour and quality of the clothes signify the group's rank in the local hierarchy.

Kajal-lagana: The bridegroom's elder brother's wife applies collyrium to the eyes of the bridegroom before the *nikashi* procession. She applies it to one eye and asks for a gift. The bridegroom is expected to present a gift ranging from Re 1 to Rs 100 or an article of equal value. As soon as she receives the gift, collyrium is applied to the other eye. The rite is known as *kajal lagana*.

Anchal-dena: Anchal-dena is a rite common among all twice-born castes and the Mali and Kachhi. It is started by the bridegroom's sister when she stops him at the door before he leaves the house to bring the bride. She is then offered a *lugada* (scarf) or a cash gift ranging up to Rs 2. Thereafter, the women assembled to witness the ceremony sprinkle cottonseed and barley over the bridegroom to compliment him. The mother of the bridegroom offers her breast to him and the bridegroom responds to this by making a gesture of respect to his mother and other elderly kin. The ceremony indicates that the bridegroom shall not defy the milk of his mother; he will uphold her honour and the honour of his family. It is traditionally acknowledged in Rajasthan that warriors leaving for battle never returned without victory, so when a bridegroom leaves home to seek the hand of his bride, he is not expected to return without the bride.

The *nikashi* procession leads to the formation of a *barat*, (the marriage party), which is a selected group of kinsmen, members of the subcaste, caste and friends. The number may vary from fifteen to two hundred depending upon the family's economic and ritual status. A Brahmin would not join a *barat* of the castes included in VII, VIII and IX divisions and vice-versa. But with the gradual weakening of caste barriers, a *barat* of a higher caste may be joined by a Bairagi or Nath, but not by a Chamar or a Bhangi. The *barats* of divisions VIII and IX are not joined by any other caste groups. The marriage parties of higher castes are usually quite heterogeneous, while other caste groups, the Rajputs, a few subcastes of the Mahajan, and the Kayastha do not allow their women to join the *barat* parties, but the women of the other castes join the men in singing, dancing and other merriment. Bullock-carts are the most common means of transportation, although automobiles have begun to be used for longer distances. Arrangements for the *barat*'s lodging are made by the bride's family at a *janwasa.*

Agvani-Karna

When a *barat* comes from another village, it stays at the outskirts of the village until a formal reception is accorded it by the bride's party. Among the higher castes some refreshments are served. Among the lower castes both parties sit down and relax and share liquor and smoke pipes while the members of the bride's party sprinkle *gulal* (colour) upon them. This activity is called *agvani karna.*

Ghar Dekhana

The arrival of the *barat* is announced by the groom's Nai to the bride's family, and a procession of people firing hand guns and exploding fireworks, headed by a band of musicians or drummer, enters the village. The Bhangi, the Chamar, and the Kachhi have their own band of musicians composed of caste members while all other castes above division VIII are served by the local band of Muslim musicians. The adorned bridegroom, riding on a mare and followed by his *barat*, takes a round of the main streets of the village and approaches the bride's house where the people of her party have assembled for the reception. At the gate of the house the bridegroom is offered sweets and an elderly married woman of the bride's family marks a *tilak* on his forehead while the bride and her friends watch the bridegroom through their transparent veils. This ceremony, called *ghardekhana*, is declining in popularity and is now observed only by the twice-born caste groups.

Badhavo-Bhejana

It is customary for the bride and groom to offer each other gifts before the wedding. The presents sent by the bridegroom's family to the bride are known as *badhavo* and include jewellery, clothes, sweets, fruits and cosmetics. These are arranged in plates and taken to the bride's house by the Nai and his wife who are led by the drummer. Similarly the groom receives gifts from the bride's family called *badhavo*, which may include a set of clothes, some dry fruits and ornaments such as a necklace, a ring, or a wrist watch. At the bride's place these presents are arranged for display before the wedding and are worn by the bride during the ceremony.

Tel-Halad-Snan

A pre-nuptial bath called the *Tel-halad-snan* is taken by the bride at her home and by the bridegroom where his *barat* is lodged. Both are assisted by the Nai and his wife who traditionally receive the clothing the couple discard for the bath. The ritual bath is preceeded by a shampoo with turmeric and perfumed oil.

Immediately after the bath the father of the bride worships the feet of the bridegroom in a ceremony called *paon-puja*. In the absence of the father of the bride, the person who will perform the *kanyadan* ceremony officiates at this rite. Re 1 is dropped in the plate of worship by the bridegroom which goes to the Nai who assists during this ritual.

Toran-Marana

After the ritual bath and the *paon puja* a procession led by the drummer or a musical band takes the bridegroom and his *barat* around the village.

The house of the bride is gaily decorated with lights, coloured flags, balloons, colored strips of paper and cloth and mural paintings. The *toran*, a wooden pentagon bearing figures of birds and sometimes a crude picture of a deity, is the symbol of the power of the bride's family. It hangs above the door flanked by the clay models of an elephant and a horse known as *chenvarian*. The bridegroom, riding a mare, arrives with the procession headed by the musical band at the *muhurt* of the *toran-marana* ceremony. Men and women gather to witness the ceremony. The bridegroom touches the *toran* with a sword or a spear and thereafter stands on a wooden plank placed over a decorative design known as *paguliva*. Fire crackers, fireworks, and hand guns are used to celebrate the occasion. The band, the drummer, and the *shahnai* players give their best performance.

Grah-Pravesh

The admission of the bridegroom into the house of the bride for the first time is known as *grah-pravesh*. When the bridegroom dismounts the horse and stands at the entrance of the house of the bride all the womenfolk welcome him. The mother of the bride performs *arti*, a ritual in which she moves a lamp in front of the bridegroom's face in a slow circular motion. This ritual, which also often accompanies the worship of the gods, conveys a warm welcome to the groom and a hope that he will bring blessings to his bride. The bride's mother then offers him sweets and performs *varana* (a gesture of respect) by moving her hands from her head to the bridegroom's head several times. The bridegroom responds by putting a rupee in the plate of worship which goes to the Nai's wife.

After the *toran-marana* ceremony the family priest arranges all the articles for *homa*. Then the bride joins the bridegroom beneath the *mandap*. Her face is veiled and she speaks softly. She sits to the right of the bridegroom, with her parents seated on her right. The priest faces the bridal couple and recites *mantras* which invoke all the gods and deities to attend and repel the malevolent spirits. He also utters a few hymns to ask the gods and deities to receive the bridal couple.

Then the priest pronounces the names of the bride and the bridegroom and of their parents and recites *mantras* to introduce them to the deities. The priest invokes the gods and deities to shower their choicest blessings upon the bridal couple while the couple glance slyly at each other and the wedding guests listen reverently.

Gath-Joda Bandhana

A husband and wife must perform all the sacred rites together or the rite is considered incomplete. Therefore, for all sacred purposes, couples are bound together with a piece of cloth called a *pachhewara*. Turmeric pieces and small betel-nuts hang from the end of the *pachhewara* of the parental couple and of the bridal couple. The bridal couple is bound together in a rite known as *gath-joda bandhana*.

Pani-Grahan

Certain marriage rites are the essence of the *samskaras* and without these a marriage is incomplete. *Panigrahan* (taking the hand of the bride), *homa* (lighting the sacred fire), and *phere* (going around the fire) are three such rites. Their elaborateness differs greatly among castes. For these rites the erected *manda* booth is consecrated and members of the family, kin group, caste and friends assemble around the booth. The bride is brought into physical contact with the bridegroom for the first time when their hands are bound with a crimson cloth and viscous myrtle is poured between their palms. The colour of the bride's palm is later examined by her girl friends, which is said to be suggestive of the intensity of love between the couple.

The Homa

The floor of the booth is plastered with red clay and cow-dung upon which is painted a *chowk* design with white clay, *kum-kum*, myrtle, rice, and wheat-flour is used to make a plaid design to decorate the *homa* brazier. The nuptial fire is lighted before the gods and deities whose idols are placed on a wooden plank. The twice-born caste groups occasionally use two or three priests to make the ceremony quite elaborate, and recite the *shlokas* (verses) in union. But only one Brahmin priest pronounces the solemn Sanskrit verses. A mixture of incense, barley, *gur*, sugar, sesame, and *ghee* is burned at each stage of the *mantras*.

Phere

The bridal couple circles the *manda* rod and the sacrificial fire seven times to perform the rite of *phere* which ritually completes the marriage. The bridal couple is joined by the bride's parents, aunts and uncles. The group is led by the bridegroom. The maternal uncle of the bride carries her around the *manda* rod on his back, and also performs the *kanyadan* ceremony. This rite seems to have originated when child marriages were common but is widely observed today. The *muhurt*, the auspicious hour of the wedding, is based upon astronomical calculations and may fall at any time of the day or night. Therefore, punctuality is maintained looking to the importance of the ceremony. All the elderly kinsmen of the bride keep a fast known as *khanal*, which is broken only after the *kanyadan* ceremony is over. The observance of this fast is limited to twice-born caste groups and is gradually becoming obsolete. Among the artisan and agricultural castes only the parents of the bride keep the fast.

Kanyadan

The bridal couple, the bride's parents and the priest take positions under the booth around the sacred fire for the rite of *kanyadan*. The priest seeks the consent of the bride's parents if they are willing to offer the *dan* (ritual gift) of their daughter to the bridegroom. He then begins chanting sacred *mantras*. While he is chanting, the bride's father drops water, rice, *kum-kum* and a few coins near the *homa* fire, signifying he is willing to give his daughter to the bridegroom. The paternal uncles and aunts of the bride may join the ceremony by touching the right hand of the parental couple with their right hand. In the absence of the father, either the elder brother, an uncle or a guardian of the girl performs this ceremony. Giving a *kanya's* hand or her *dan* is considered among the holiest acts in the life of a parent.

During the *kanyadan* ceremony, *hathleva* (gifts) are presented to the bride by the adult members of the family, caste and friends. All the dresses, cash, ornaments, utensils and furniture she receives form the *dahej* (dowry). The cost of all the articles reflects the prestige of the bride's family. A kin, while performing the rite of *hathleva*, puts his gift, some water and *kum-kum* in his right hand and drops it in the brass plate. The bridegroom's representative, usually the maternal uncle, the elder sister's husband or the father's sister's husband collects all the articles and lists the gifts and their contributors. The value of the gifts varies greatly from caste to caste. Among the twice-born caste groups it may vary from two hundred rupees to a few thousand rupees but among the artisan and agricultural castes it does not exceed a few hundred rupees. The lowest castes, such as the Mer, Bola, Balai and the Bnangi, do not observe the ceremony at all.

Sakshi-Karana

Following the *kanyadan* ceremony, the priest recites a few verses and stresses the permanence of the marital bond as decreed in sacred principles. He instructs the bridal couple to make certain vows before the sacred fire, the gods, and the assembled guests to make their domestic life a success by mutual love and cooperation. This rite is called *sakshi-karana* (witnessing).

Dakshina

The priest who conducts the wedding ceremony is offered a *dakshina* (gift) by the parents of the bride. Though the amount of the *dakshina* is fixed by the priest himself, it is in good taste to pay more than the priest asks. The twice-born caste groups usually pay the priest Rs 25 for a girl's marriage and Rs 30 for a boy's marriage. Members of the artisan and agricultural castes give the priest Rs 15. The amount ranges from Rs 10 to Rs 15 among the lower castes. Before receiving the *dakshina*, the priest marks the *tilak* on the forehead of the bride's father and the bridegroom and on the bracelets of the left hand of the bride and her mother. He then receives a small gift of cash and a coconut.

Devi-Devata Pooja

After completing the ceremonies under the *manda* booth, the bridal couple worship the gods and deities of the bride's family and pray for blessings, prosperity and the well-being of the partners. The father's sister or the elder sister of the bride tells the bridal couple what they must do during various phases of the worship. She is assisted by the Nai of the family who receives the offerings made to the deities.

Goran

On the day following the wedding a large dinner called the *goran* is arranged for the groom's party. This is a grand feast to which all friends, the caste, neighbourhood and other castes are invited. A wide variety of delicacies are prepared. The number of dishes indicates the status of the bride's family. The bridegroom is seated with his male friends and joins the dinner after receiving a gift from the bride's father which may range from a rupee to an article costing Rs 2 to Rs 3. It is a festive occasion which finds the groom's party teasing and joking with the members of the bride's party. Laughter and merriment prevail. A group of women sing *galian*, humorous songs which describe the bridegroom's relatives and friends. The *Rao-bhat* (the minstrel of the family) narrates poetically for the guests the family's history, its development in relation to the caste, and lineage. After the dinner the bridegroom puts a rupee or two in the dinner plate for the Nai. The *goran* of the non-twice-born castes have a tendency to become somewhat rowdy at times. The singing and dancing, accompanied by a great deal of noisy ribald humour, continues into the early hours of the morning. Among the agricultural castes which allow themselves to indulge in intoxicating beverages, the situation occasionally gets completely out of hand. Arguments and fist-fights have a way of cropping up and often the *goran* ends in the wee hours as a drunken brawl. The Dhobi are especially notorious for their festive escapades which at times assume riotous proportions.

Kanwar-Kaleva

On the morning following the wedding day, the bridegroom is invited with his friends for his *kaleva* (breakfast) at the bride's residence. Sumptuous dishes of sweets, vegetables, sauces and *namkins* are served on a large plate, arranged on a wooden plank which is placed in the centre of the *manda* booth. The guests sit around the food plate and the bridegroom waits for the ceremonial gift. The gift may be a gold necklace, a wrist watch, a ring or even a radio. No gift is given among the other castes except the twice-born. The frivolity is assumed to promote amity between the parties. Odd things like cotton threads are mixed in the food, which causes the guests to eat cautiously. When the bridegroom is engrossed in his breakfast, a younger brother of the bride or the sister sneaks off with his shoes, returning them only after much teasing, coaxing, and the receipt of a small reward. *Kanwar-kaleva* is popular among the Brahmin and the Mahajan. However, among the Rajput, the bridegroom joins his bride as he stays with her during the rest of the ceremonies.

Milani

The kinsmen and friends of the bride and the bridegroom are formally introduced to one another through a ceremony known as *milani*. The bridegroom is seated and offered a special set of clothes, some cash, and dry fruits by the oldest male member of the bride's party. *Patasha* and dry fruits are distributed among the people assembled. Among the artisan and agricultural castes the bridegroom receives no cash. The Brahmin officiates at the occasion. When the introductions begin, the people involved stand up, fold their hands and exchange the *tilak* mark. The person from the bride's family offers from Re 1 to Rs 100 to his counterpart. The amount presented varies according to the position of the individual in the kin group.

While this practice can be very costly for the bride's family, it has always been considered a mark of prestige. The twice-born caste groups are beginning to eliminate money gifts from this ceremony.

Jua-Khelana

To help the bridal couple overcome their shyness and nervousness, they play a ceremonial game called *jua khelana* at midday. Before the game starts the couple unties the seven knotted *kankan-doras*. Light-coloured turmeric water is poured into a large bowl beneath the marriage booth. A silver or gold ring which is given by the bridegroom's brother-in-law, and some articles such as betel-nut, seeds of tamarind, a ring of lac, and some leaves of grass are mixed in the water, and the bridal couple both try to fish out the golden ring. Whoever finds the ring wins a point. This may be repeated ten to fifteen times. All young women are divided into two groups, one assisting the bridegroom and the other the bride, while some of the *baratis* witness the game. A group of women sing hints to the players intermittently to aid their search. A woman, usually the bride's brother's wife, acts as a referee. The game creates a humorous situation as the couple find each other's fingers under the water more often than they find the ring. More often than not it is the bride who wins in this game even though she plays with her face veiled.

Khetrapal

The Khetrapal ceremony is the local term for the worship of the godling who protects the village. The bridal couple, a group of women, a drummer, and the Nai who bears the plate of worship materials, walk to the boundary of the village. Since there is no distinct shrine of Kshetrapal, the Nai arranges a few stone godlings beneath a tree and directs the couple in the worship. It is believed that the propitiation of the godlings is necessary to obtain blessings for a prosperous married life.

Rodi-Puja

Along with the worship of Kshetrapal, a heap of dirt called *rodi* is also worshipped, implying that malevolent powers should also be propitiated along with the sacred.

Palangachar

A finely made bedstead is brought for the ceremony of *palangchar*. All the domestic utensils and other articles to be given as dowry are placed near it. The bedstead is covered with cotton, silk, or cheap velvet bedsheets, cushions, and, if required, a blanket, bedsheets, and mattresses. While the bridal couple sit on the bedstead, the mother of the bride begins the ceremony by putting a *kum-kum* mark on the forehead of the bridegroom and a bracelet on the bride. The bridegroom is expected to grasp the corner of his mother-in-law's scarf and hold it until she offers a gift, which varies from family to family. Generally it is not less than a rupee. Among the prosperous twice-born caste groups, it might be an article costing from Rs 50 to Rs 100.

Rang-Bhat

Next morning the *barat* is served with *kaccha* food. For the feast named *rang-bhat* either yellow-coloured sweet-rice preparation or *khichari* is served along with roasted wheat balls, *bati*, or *bafla* with cooked pulses, vegetables and *chutney*.

Tuntiya

During the stay of a *barat* in the bride's village, the caste and neighbourhood arrange a *tuntiya* (mock marriage) in the house of the bridegroom by the women of the kin group. This practice is prevalent in the twice-born caste groups since they do not allow their women to join the *barat* parties. On the day of the wedding the women are invited to celebrate the *tuntiya* rite. One woman plays the role of the bridegroom and some other of the bride and in a similar way important roles are assigned. The bridal couple, thus formed, performs all the ceremonies in a summarised way. The performance is entertaining and thoroughly enjoyed by the women.

Barat-ki-Bidai

The zeal of the parties gradually decreases as the ceremonies come to an end and finally the groom's party has to bid farewell. A formal departure is made conspicuous by offering a coconut, a rupee, a tumbler, bowl or plate, or a combination of these gifts to the *baratis*. On this occasion the bride weeps as she joins another family, but the grief of the family is compensated by the joy of giving the girl in marriage. The tears are mixed with a great consolation and joy. The father of the bride instructs her to assist her new parents and other family members faithfully. Her docility, submissiveness and judiciousness are appreciated but the father of the bride requests her father-in-law to pardon her faults and failings. The drummer or the musical band heads the procession and the people of the village, the members of the family, and the relatives come to see off the party to the outskirts of the village. The servants who looked after the comforts of the *barat* party of twice-born castes are rewarded in cash. Twice-born castes also send a younger relative or a maid with the bride to help her set up her new household.

After the wedding rites at the bride's home the rituals at the groom's home take place. This series of rites relates to the incorporation of the bride into the groom's family and kin group, and the acceptance and recognition of the groom as a new member of the bride's family.

Most of the following discussion relates to post-wedding rituals observed by the Brahmin and Mahajan caste groups. Differences in other castes, whenever significant, are also dealt with.

The departure of the groom's party is a sad occasion for the departing bride and her family, but after the pressure of several days of marriage ceremonies, it comes as something of a relief. The bride's family accompanies her to the outskirts of the village and the women sing farewell songs and her parents ask that her shortcomings be overlooked. When the *barat* of an upper caste party departs, the bride's family offers some packages of sweets known as *lavana* to the groom's father. These sweets are distributed among friends, neighbours, and caste members. The family Nai assists in the distribution and receives some grain from each family in return. After a tearful farewell the bride's family returns home and the bride begins the journey to her husband's village.

Pavano-ki-Bidai (*Farewell to Guests*)

Gradually all the ceremonies are completed and the *pavana* (guests) return to their respective villages. The closest relatives and friends receive a *bidai* (ceremonial farewell). Each man receives a *tilak* mark on his forehead and the women are marked on the bracelet of their left hand. The bride's father gives a gift ranging from Re 1 to Rs 5 with a coconut to each departing kin or friend. Each guest also receives some clothing which is delivered to the person's home after he returns. The quantity and quality varies with the intensity of the relationship. Occasionally, departing kinsmen and guests are also presented with packets of sweets.

When the bride arrives in her husband's village it is very likely she will find herself faced with a number of crotchets. For example, it is believed that a girl from a rich family will be a poor cook and a lax housekeeper. A girl with an education is believed to be disobedient and a girl from a larger town is thought to be more concerned with her clothing and make-up than her responsibilities at home.

The groom's parties have their own means of transport. Parties which come a long distance usually take buses, but the agricultural and lower castes ride bullock-carts. In some cases the groom's party walks while the bride and the bridegroom ride on horseback or in a bullock-cart. Among the Brahmin, Rajput, Mahajan, and Kayastha, the women join these parties and visit the bride's home. After the wedding an escort accompanies the bride to her new home.

Ghar-me-lena (*Reception of the Bridal Couple*)

When the groom returns to his village with his bride, they must wait at the bus stop, a friend's place or a temple until they are taken to their formal reception. The procession to the reception travels through the centre of the village while women gather at the groom's house to greet the couple.

When they arrive the bridegroom stands at the right side of the bride and an agnatic married woman performs *tanak-toda* (a magical rite of measuring the bride and the bridegroom seven times with a piece of multicoloured thread). Then the couple are taken to the room of the deities for worship. During these and the following ceremonies the bride follows the groom in all the ritual activities. The Nai washes the plate containing the worship materials and receives his *neg*. Except for the Gosain, Bairagi, Nath and Kalal, the Nai does not render services to the castes of divisions VII, VIII, and IX on this occasion.

Patasha or *gur* is distributed to the women who participate on this occasion. The groom's sister stands at the entrance of the house and performs the ritual of *darwaja-rokana*. She stands at the door and allows everyone to enter except her brother and his bride. To gain admittance the groom puts in the plate of worship a few coins ranging from Rs 2 to Rs 20 and sometimes a gift such as a ring or necklace. Occasionally a gift for each of the groom's sisters is put in the plate but more often one sister receives a gift and the others divide the cash. In one Brahmin marriage, more than 100 rupees were divided among three sisters following the *darwaja-rokana* rite. But among the Kachhi and Mer each sister usually receives only two rupees.

Devata-Puja (*Worship of Deities*)

After entering the home of the bridegroom, the couple worships the Ganesh deity at the place where he was invoked during the *bindyak-baithana* ceremony. The Brahmin priest directs couples of the twice-born castes in this worship. The Nai's wife directs the couple of all other castes except those belonging to the VIII and IX divisions. The mother, aunts, and sisters of the groom witness the ceremony while the women of the caste and neighbour-hood sing devotional and marriage songs. The priest who officiates at the worship is given a rupee and a coconut in *dakshina*. The Nai and the drummer each receive 50 paise and some grain as a ritual gift. The women assembled for the ceremony are given *patashas* or *gur*.

Muha-Dekhana (*Reception of the Bride*)

Throughout the course of the marriage the bride's face is covered with a crimson scarf which is a part of her wedding dress. She acts very shy and speaks softly and to none except young children and her attendants. Even while drinking water she keeps her face covered, holding the glass under the veil. She is expected to follow these norms until she becomes a mother and begins sharing responsibilities with her mother-in-law.

During the *muha-dekhana* ritual each of the groom's female relations lifts the bride's veil for their first look of the new member of the family. Even the groom must wait until this ceremony for his first look at his bride's face, which takes place in a locked room. The women from the caste and neighbourhood come to see the face of the bride and present her with a small gift. The bride sits in the verandah or a receiving room and the women approach her one at a time to peep under the veil. The bride is expected to pay respects to all elderly women in her new family.

On the bride's first visit to her natal family, she is usually asked about the gift given her by her mother-in-law and her husband. The gift is believed to be a reliable index of the class and prestige of the groom's family. Even though among the lower castes the rite of *muha-dikhana* is not given much significance, the gift given by the mother-in-law is highly valued. Such gifts become a common subject of discussion among the women during their leisure hours.

The adult brides and grooms anxiously await the first time they will be alone and discuss matters with their close peers. Mature grooms seek advice from their experienced friends on making advances to their new mates, as do the brides. Almost all young married people seek advice and direction from close friends in matters connected with sex. In the domestic surrounding girls are gradually taught to refrain from meeting other young men in private. They are instructed that an ideal wife can only think of one man in her lifetime, her husband. The girl learns the behaviour expected of her in her conjugal home from the women of her natal family. Girl friends of her own age group provide her with knowledge of sexual matters and caution her regarding the treatment of her conjugal kin group and their probable reactions to her failings and virtues. The ideal bride should be meek, submissive, tolerant and obedient and should not enter into controversy with her husband or his family.

Rati-Jaga

The night of the *barat's* return to the groom's village is the first that the bridal couple spend together. This is called the *rati-jaga* ceremony. Rajput bridegrooms observe the ritual of *rati-jaga* at the bride's house the night following the wedding. After the worship of the deities during the night, the rite of *rati-jaga* takes place. The ritual of *rati-jaga* involves the consumation of the marriage. The rite begins with the detention of the bridal couple in a room, usually the cell of *bindyak*. The groom's aunts or sisters-in-law arrange things for the ceremony. They prepare the bedstead on the bed given to the bride in marriage, put sweets, betel-leaves, and a jar of water in the room, and ask the bride to relax there. The bridegroom is then asked to bring an article from the room. As soon as he enters the room, the doors are bolted from outside. Although most of the bridal couples understand this cultural pattern, they shyly pretend to resist these efforts. In cases of child-couples such detention is not encouraged since they do not understand the significance of the event.

While the bridal couple are detained in the room, the bridegroom is expected to initiate a modest conversation with the bride. According to traditional norms the bride is not supposed to yield to his advances and is expected to be shy and bashful. The groom gradually makes more daring advances and gently removes the veil. She tries to resist his efforts and attempts to keep her face covered until she receives a gift from him. Tradition demands that the husband must wield authority, and command respect and obedience from his wife. The groom uses this superiority to his advantage.

The room selected for *rati-jaga* is usually in a central position in the house, which affords the young couple little privacy. Even their conversation must be in a low whisper. In cases of adult bridal couples, the young married kinswomen, who are usually on joking terms with the couple, comment indirectly on the pleasures derived by the couple's first meeting, particularly in their sexual act.

The agricultural, artisan, and the lower castes enjoy singing and dancing on this occasion. They trade jibes and lewd jests with one another as they dance to the rhythm of a drum. The Kumhar, Dhobi, Khatik, Balai, Mer and the Bola serve liquor on this occasion, while the Dhakar, Kachhi and Mali may have liquor but the host is not obliged to offer it. The celebration continues long into the night, and it is not unusual for the food prepared in the morning to be ignored until the following day, in favour of liquor. The Dholi collects Rs 5 to Rs 10 as a gift from the patrons. The *nyochhavar* money is given to the Dholi after the performance of *varana* by waving a coin over the head of the dancer.

Before the bride returns to her natal home, *binora* feasts are organised by her husband's kinsmen and friends (see Chapter 9). The bride is expected to return to her parental home after staying at her new home a week or two. Among the Brahmin, the Rajput and the Mahajan, either a younger sister, a brother, or the family Nai or a domestic servant accompanies her to her new home. Three or four days after the wedding a party of the bride's kinsmen and the family Nai reaches the bridegroom's village to escort the bride on her return. Among the agricultural castes, the Dhakar, the Kachhi and the Mali, from two to ten men act as escorts. Among the castes of divisions VIII and IX, the Nai or any other assistant does not join the party. The upper castes prefer that a younger brother serve as a bride's escort since the elder members customarily are prohibited from being entertained at the bride's conjugal house. Traditionally, any member older than the bride should not even accept water at her conjugal home. In past times, such members refused even water from a well of the groom's village. Now, however, either arrangements for such guests are made at the house of some other member of the caste, or a nominal payment is made for the comforts provided by the groom's family. Visitors of the agricultural and lower castes either carry food with them or buy it from the village market and prepare their meals separately. Intra-village marriages have weakened the rigidity of this custom.

When the bride departs for her natal home, the groom's family is expected to give her a set of clothes if they belong to an upper caste, and several sets of clothes to her younger brothers and sisters. If the person who comes to take the bride back is older than her, he has to give Rs 2 to Rs 5 to the children of the groom's family. If he is the bride's father or grandfather, he has to present Rs 2 to Rs 11 to the groom's father. If the groom's grandfather is alive, he receives even more than the father.

The groom receives such cash gifts from all senior members of the bride's kingroup during his subsequent visits to her home or on other formal occasions. In return, he offers a smaller cash gift to their children. This arrangement serves to strengthen the kin ties.

The Nai acts as the regular attendant for any guests the family receives and serves them during their visits. He receives one or two rupees or some of the visitors' used clothing.

The bride's journey to or from her natal home necessitates a formal attire which symbolises her new marital status. She has her hair done and wears her best ceremonial dress and jewellery. She also decorates her hands and feet with myrtle, or rose water if she is from a lower caste.

A set of rites which concludes the marriage ceremonies is known as *gauna*. The *gauna* ceremony takes place in the bride's village when her husband returns to take her back to his home to live with him permanently. *Gauna* may take place anytime from six months to seven years after the marriage, depending mainly on the ages of the newly married couple. The *gauna* rite signals the consummation of a child marriage; in the case of an adult marriage it is merely a brief formal ceremony. For the boys of higher castes *Chatara-chauth* or *Ganesh-chauth* is a major festival. The girl's family is expected to send him *danda-ladoo* (a pair of sticks and balls of fried gram and sugar), a set of clothes, a pen and ink and possibly some cash. The expenditure varies from Rs 50 to Rs 250. *Ladoos* (sweets) are distributed among the families of the caste and friends.

If the bride is living at the groom's home during the month of Shravana (July-August) when the festival of Teej occur, the parents of the bride are expected to send *satu* (balls of fried wheat flour, rice, gram mixed with ghee and sugar). If the bride has been staying at her natal home, *satu* is sent to the groom's family to be distributed among the families of the caste and the neighbourhood. The poorer caste families send token cash gifts ranging from Rs 5 to Rs 11. The groom's family is expected to send the bride's family a *laharia* (a colourfully striped scarf), sweets, some cash, and cosmetics during the month of Shravana.

After the marriage the bride begins observing a married woman's rituals by worshipping the deities and observing fasts with great sanctity, which may bless her with a long married life.

Devi-Devataon-ki-Bidai

The gods and deities, who are considered to be the protectors of the clan, lineage and family are worshipped faithfully from the first day of the marriage. Hardly a ritual exists in which the god and deities are not reverently entreated. The castes of the first six divisions (see Table 1) bring the family deities from their abodes for the ceremonies and return them after the marriage. Occasionally, these castes organise a feast for the sole purpose of worshipping the family deity. The offerings made to the deity go either to the married sister, the bride's father's sisters, or the Brahmin priests.

Family life in Awan has retained its rural character with families either living off their small pieces of land or earning their livelihood by rendering services to other groups. Social contacts of the family as a unit are usually confined to members of the kin group, people of the neighbourhood and members of the caste living in the locality, with only occasional contacts with caste members from neighbouring villages and towns.

The term *parivar* or *ghar* (family) is used in several contexts and may refer to any number of people related to one another by varying degrees. The *khas parivar* or *mool parivar* (nuclear family) includes a parental couple and their children. The *bada parivar* or *bada ghar* (joint family) includes agnatic kinsmen. It generally embraces four to five living generations and can be demarcated by definable limits. The *bada parivar* differs distinctly from the *kutumb* since *kutumb* includes bilateral kin groups (cf. Mayer 1960: 169-171).

The *bada parivar* is a group composed of a number of family units living in separate apartments of the same house who eat food cooked at one hearth, share a common income and common property, and are related to one another through agnatic kinship such as a man and his sons, grandsons, or a set of brothers, their sons and grandsons. The women of the household are their wives, unmarried daughters, and perhaps the widow of a deceased kinsman. They participate in common family worship and share mutual rights and responsibilities (Stevenson 1920: 58; O'Malley 1934: 122; Srinivas 1942: 22; Desai, I.P. 1956: 147-148).

While structurally the *parivar* or *ghar* as the smallest unit and the *bada parivar* or *bada ghar* as the largest unit of a family exist together, the eldest male, often the father, administers the family funds. His wishes and decisions are rarely challenged by his sons. Traditionally he manages the family affairs and acts as its spokesman. The women have no rights over the family property while their husbands are living.

Since Awan is primarily an agricultural community, the joint family is both a consuming and a producing unit. All the family members work in the fields and share the produce. While a male member of the family may work in the fields of anyone in the village, he must pool his income with that of the joint family.

There are occasions when members of a joint family break away into smaller units, due to some dispute or differences, and establish their kitchens separately. However, loyalties to the joint family are often re-established on the occasion of religious ceremonies and functions. A marriage is the most common occasion for such members to be drawn back into the family and participate once again in the common family enterprise.

A family which shares a common dwelling does not necessarily function as a joint family. To become a joint family, it must share, among other things, the social and economic responsibilities of marriages which take place in the family. Therefore, it is necessary to understand the role each member of the family unit plays in a marriage.

A person's kinsmen are all those with whom he is geneologically connected through his father, mother and his wife. This kinship relation is referred to as *lagtika*; every individual in the configuration of kinship is a *lagtika*. The nature of the relationship between two people determines the role expectations. Since the village has an intense web of kinship within it as a result of village endogamy, a person marrying within the village may have several kin ties with a particular individual. During a marriage all *lagtika* members have a specific role they are expected to play. In case a particular individual is not available to perform a ritual role, a distant relative is asked to perform the role. This substitution makes it possible to incorporate even the *durka* (distant kins) of the *lagtika* group into a family's marriage rituals.

In cases where a joint family in some aspects is no longer functioning as a joint family, ceremonial occasions serve to unite them again. For example, a family said to be a joint family may no longer share a common income or even live together. But occasions such as births, deaths or marriages necessitate that they achieve a certain degree of ritual congruence which eventually reinforces unity in the fizzling joint family. Each nuclear family may have achieved a degree of self-sufficiency as an independent unit, but they remain dependent upon one another as a ritual unit. Due to the change in the family structure from the joint to the nuclear family, which is taking place among the twice-born castes, the father of the child is gradually beginning to make decisions independent of the aid of the older generation of kinsmen. A great deal of authority in the non-twice-born castes remains in the hands of the kinsmen and caste members.

Along with the kinsmen, many fellow villagers participate in certain rites. Business partners, friends or neighbours may sometimes be closer to the family than some relatives. The extent of the relationship is illustrated by the importance of the role the person is asked to perform. A person's importance is also determined by the number of roles he performs. Multiple roles being performed by the same individual in a wedding is a strong indication of the person's importance to the bride or groom and their respective families.

Strained relationships often result when a relative fails to properly perform his role in a wedding ceremony. The mode of reciprocity among the kinsmen entails a system of persistence upon which the relationships and the solidarity of the kin group are based. Deviations in the performance of duties and failure to offer one's service at the designated occasions lead to quarrels and strained relationships. While many factors tend to draw a family apart, it is considered disgraceful if a family is unable to unite in crisis situations, including weddings.

To insure the degree of unity required to properly perform a marriage, relatives of the family and the members of the caste meet to examine their solidarity. At these occasions members of the joint family and kin group openly air their grievances and discuss points of conflict with one another.

Members of the family are obliged to perform certain rituals which help maintain the kinship unity. Renewing these ties serves to strengthen the effectiveness of the kin group organisation. Before a marriage the members of the kin group outside the nuclear family are extended formal verbal or written invitations. This formally informs them of the new alliance the family is making and the consequent putative kinship extensions.

Purity and Pollution

Under certain circumstances a person or a family loses its sacred status of purity and becomes polluted. Births and deaths are considered profane and pollute a family for a fixed period of time, depending on the family's caste. However, occasionally a sacred event will take place during a period of pollution, such as a marriage taking place soon after a death. In these situations the sacred prevails over the profane. For example, a Brahmin family is usually considered contaminated for forty days after the birth of a child. But if a marriage is to take place during this time, the period may be shortened to only a week.

A death also pollutes the members of the family for a specific period of time. Among the twice-born caste groups, a family declares a two-week period of mourning. The castes of divisions VI, VII, and some of division VIII remain polluted for thirteen days. The remainder of group VIII (the Meena, Bhil, Nayak) and the castes in division IX declare they are once again pure on the eleventh day. Observance of the rites of mourning are as essential as the rites of marriage, and the people observe all the obsequies with necessary details so that the soul of the dead may not remain unpropitiated. If the *muhurt* (span of auspiciousness) for the marriage falls within a week after a death in the family the rites go on simultaneously. An individual who performs *kriya-karma* and *pinda-dan* or *katta*, the ceremonies which propitiate the spirit of the dead, is prohibited from participating in marriage rites and must remain secluded. If the *lagan-patra* (marriage letter) was received before the death occurred, the wedding is still solemnised on the stipulated day. Marriages which take place under such circumstances are not looked down upon. They are viewed instead as the replacing of a departed member of the family with a new person. For the people of Awan the cardinal principle of life is that sorrow must ultimately be transformed into rejoicing.

The death of a family member at the time of a marriage brings the profane and sacred into conflict. Superstition once blamed the bride, as a new member, for bringing ill-luck to the family, especially if the death was unexpected.

The solemnisation of a marriage is not generally postponed if a distant relation or a person in the mother's natal family dies. Also, a marriage must be solemnised if the preliminaries for the wedding have already taken place. Generally the period of mourning ends a year later when the last purificatory ritual of death known as *barasi* has been performed. Marriages which are to take place within a year of the death of a member of the family are postponed. In situations when preliminary rites of marriage have taken place the *barasi* ritual may be summarised so that the marriage may be completed. However, most twice-born, artisan, and agricultural castes frown upon such a compendious approach.

The age of the deceased is also considered when determining the length of the mourning period. An infant's death pollutes the members for only a month, but the death of an older person pollutes the family for as long as a year.

The subject of ritual participation becomes very complex when considering the underlying implications of the rituals. This discussion examines the twice-born castes in detail, mentioning the lower castes only when the deviation from the twice-born castes is significant. The rigid structure of the rituals and the intricate interrelationships between people which the rituals depict can be understood by describing the role played by each individual in the marriage.

THE ROLE OF THE FATHER

Awan is a village composed of patri-families and the father is the chief patriarch of the family. He is the person who makes all arrangements for the marriages of his children and shares the economic responsibilities. From the day he begins searching for a spouse for his child, he is responsible for every detail of the marriage. He participates in all rituals except those which are traditionally for women or the bridal couple only. By participating he asserts his position in the family and approves of the marriage his child is about to make.

In the sub-cultural region of Harauti, four terms are used to mean father—*bhaiji, pitaji, kakaji, babuji*. The first term, which is now in vogue, may have entered usage when young children, who used *bhai* to address an older brother, added *ji*, a mark of respect, to address their father. The term *pitaji* is apparently nominative of the Sanskrit work *pitra* and is popular among the literate families. The use of the term *kakaji* is the outcome of two processes: (*i*) the term is learned by the children who imitate the term used by the children of their father's elder brother for their father's younger brothers. (*ii*) A child of a non-twice-born caste group distinguishes between his real father and the man his mother remarries. It also symbolises the custom of levirate. A stepfather is called *kaka* or *kakaji*. The term *babuji* is popular only among the service classes, who have been influenced by the process of urbanisation.

For the performance of rites and ceremonies, a stepfather has the same legal and ritual status as a real father. In the absence of the father his brother may take his place in the rituals.

The role of the father is acknowledged in the *tilak* ceremony. Even if the father is deceased his name remains in the formal recitations, spells or *mantras*, declarations, and announcements.

During the *sagai* of a boy, presents are given to the father. Both the groom and his father receive a *saropav*, indicating the father as the most important man in the total network of social ties.

The father of a girl sends the *lagan* letter to the bridegroom's family. He is the chief participant in the *bindyak-baithana* ceremony. Organising the *binori* processions is also a part of his duties. He receives the guests, accepts presents of *passi* from them, and keeps a record of the presents. The invitations for the feast of *manda* are sent in his name. With his wife he participates in the *mandal-baithana* ceremony and receives each of his kinsmen from his wife's family. He receives the bridegroom's party and bows at the groom's feet before the *toran-marana* ceremony. He participates in the ritual of *grah-pravesh*, *homa*, *panigrahan* and *phere*.

The *kanyadan* rite, in which the daughter is given to the groom, is the principal ritual which is performed by the parental couple. Performing the rite is the highest honour a person may attain in his lifetime (Kane 1941: 440-441; Kapadia 1966:131).

At the ritual of *kunwar-kalewa* the bride's father presents either a gift or a small sum of cash to the bridegroom. The ritual is observed only by the twice-born castes. Custom declares that the bridegroom may insist on a gift of his own choosing, but usually the gift is determined by mutual agreement.

During the *palangchar* ceremony the father of the bride circles the bed seven times completing the last round by circumscribing all the articles given to his daughter in dowry. The articles are placed around the bed. The completion of the ceremony is supplemented by his offering of a *saropav*, a coconut and a few rupees, to the groom's nearest male kins.

The Maheshwari Mahajan hold a feast after the main wedding ceremonies known as *goran* at which the father of the bride presents the bridegroom with a gift for joining the dinner party. The gift is considered to be a mark of respect and locally interpreted as a dignifying gesture on the part of the bride's family. The father of the bride is expected to perform his role in accordance with the norms of the caste and the community. He is expected to be modest, courteous and humble while dealing with the bridegroom's party.

The father's role as the primary kin in his son's marriage is the result of the authority he wields in the family, particularly in handling the marriage negotiations. The father of the boy receives the *lagan* from the bride's family and puts it before the caste council to declare the initiation of marriage. He invokes the gods and deities and performs the worship of the Ganesh deity. He organises *binori* processions and participates in the *mandal-baithana* ceremony, during which he receives gifts of clothing from kinsmen and close friends. The *nikashi* procession for the departing *barat* is again managed by him. He joins his son in the *ghar-dekhana* ritual and sends gifts of clothing and jewelry to the bride. The *toran-marana* and *grah-pravesh* rituals are witnessed by him. His presence is thought to be very necessary during the performance of the main wedding rituals, even when he takes part only as an observer. He joins the *goran* and *rangbhat* feasts and the *milani* ritual. When the marriage ceremonies are complete and the *barat* leaves to return to its village with the new bride, the groom's father receives the fondest *bidai* (farewell). When they arrive again at home the father performs the *bidai* rite first for all the assembled kinsmen and guests and then for the gods and deities.

Of the 43 marriage rituals, the father of the bride participates in 18 rituals while the father of the bridegroom participates in 14 rituals. There are 10 rituals in which both fathers participate together. In comparison to the other members of the family, the father holds the major responsibilities for the marriage and thereby participates in the largest number of rituals.

THE ROLE OF THE MOTHER

While the father is responsible for all the preliminary arrangements for a marriage, the mother is responsible for the success of the wedding ceremony itself. Before the date of a marriage she remains in the background, prodding her husband to find the best possible partners for their marriageable children. The higher caste woman's knowledge of the marriage rituals is extremely thorough which insures that the rituals will be performed with great sanctity. Since the marriage of a child is so important an event in the life of a mother, no aspect of the marriage is omitted (Stevenson 1920:58). The mother remains the main chaperon for the bride and acquaints her with all her new social responsibilities and obligations.

The role of the mother is accentuated by her association and participation in the series of rituals observed during the marriage. Her authority and privileges, which are determined in domestic life only after much squabbling and bickering, are more clearly defined in the performance of her ritual roles. Of the 43 marriage rituals she actively participates in 25 rituals while her managerial responsibilities are increased in a girl's marriage. The mother of a boy participates in the following marriage rituals: *bindyak-baithana, khanagar, chari-jhakolana, basan-lana, binori, mandal-baithana, paharavani, nikashi, tuntiya, ghar-me-lana, devi-devata puja, muha-dikhai, pavano-ki-bidai* and *devataon-ki-bidai*.

The mother's role in a girl's marriage is even more extensive than her participation in rituals would indicate. Since the main wedding rites are solemnised at the bride's house, she must organise the rituals and see that they are properly performed. Beginning with the initial arrangements, the girl's mother participates in the following rituals: *bindyak-baithana, khanagar-lana, basan-lana, binori, mandal-baithana, paharavani, grah-pravesh, panigrahan, homa, phere, kanyadan, sakshi-karana, dakshina, devi-devata puja, khetarpal-puja, palangachar, barat-ki-bidai, pavano-ki-bidai, and devi-devataon-ki-bidai*.

Awan is a patriarchal community and polygyny is a popular institution among the non-twice-born castes; hence there are cases when an individual must recognise socially more than one woman as mother, since the blood relationship is predominated by social ties.

Children who live with their mother and a stepfather are called *galad*, to distinguish them from the children born from a second husband. When a *galad* is married, the ceremonies remain the same as if one were living with one's natural father. Likewise, a stepmother would take the place of a natural mother in all wedding rituals.

THE SIBLINGS

The siblings are referred to by those terms which signify their relationship, such as *bhai* for brother or *behan* for sister. However, prefixes with classificatory terms denote their positions. Like their father, the brothers of a bride or groom of a twice-born caste receive gifts of clothing, sweets, and cash at the *sagai*.

The Role of Male Siblings

The younger brother often plays the role of *bindyak* (a personification of the Ganesh deity) accompanying the bride or the bridegroom continually during the days of ritual performances until the wedding is solemnised. Upon completion of his ritual role the *bindyak* receives a gift of clothing, a coconut and a rupee. This role may also be performed by one of the male agnates, cognates, or individuals traced out to be within recognisable kinship. At one time in the absence of a brother or close male kin, a Brahmin boy was assigned this role, but now a boy from any clean caste can play the role.

The bride or groom's brothers receive gifts from their nearest kinsmen at the *mandal-baithana* and serve as hosts and entertainers for the *barat* party. At the *milani* ceremony the male siblings and the nearest agnates and the cognates of the bridegroom's side ceremonially greet their counterparts of the bride's side. Equality of status is maintained at this occasion.

The Role of Female Siblings

A girl leaves her natal family and joins the clan of her husband after her marriage but she retains her affiliation with her agnate family. The term *ben-beti* (sister-daughter) denotes any female blood relative of the family. It is assumed that all girls in the family are meant to be given away in *dan* (ritual gift). The family refuses any gift from them or their husband's family which it is not able to repay. When gifts are accepted they are returned with something more added to them.

The role of the married sisters who are separated from the family at ritual occasions is meant to preserve and revitalise the relationship which has a way of becoming weak and obscure. Their role in the performance of ritual occasions rejuvenates their relationship with their natal family.

The accepted procedure is that a married sister should be sent an invitation to a wedding and escorted from her village to the wedding by a member of the family. She is expected to attend a funeral on her own accord. Thirty to forty days before a wedding, a representative of the family, such as a male family member, the family priest or the Nai, journeys to her village to formally invite her and her family. She is expected to assist her natal family in the preliminary preparations for the marriage, such as the preparation of food, washing and decorating the house. From the day of the first invocation of the Ganesh deity, the sister performs the *arti* ceremony after all rituals and receives gifts from the brother or sister for whom the ritual is performed. The number of rituals performed by a girl is larger among the higher castes because the number of rituals which necessitate some sort of worship is larger in number.

The *binori* processions for the bride or groom which tour the main streets and village market are financed by the married sisters. This involves expenditure on a musical band, a horse, lamps, and sweets which are distributed among the participants.

The sisters also perform in the ceremony, in which they bring water to be used in the upcoming rituals from the village well in jars balanced on their head. After *mandal-baithana* and *paharavan* they perform *arti* before the seated parental couple. The *kanyadan phere* and the worship of the deities is also concluded by a performance of *arti*.

Later a younger sister or brother of the bride steals a pair of shoes of the bridegroom and returns it only when a gift is received. The custom is said to serve the purpose of bringing the bride's siblings closer to their new brother-in-law.

On the return of the *barat*, the groom's sister performs *arti* before the bridal couple before they enter the house and in a ritual called *dehl-rokana*, refuses to allow the couple to enter until she receives a gift.

The *ben-beti* are the last to leave after the conclusion of all marriage ceremonies. They are accorded a formal *bidai* (farewell), and given gifts of clothing for the members of their nuclear family and cash gifts ranging from Re 1 to Rs 5 among the higher castes and 25 to 50 paise among the agricultural castes. The children also receive similar presents and a bag of sweets at the time of their departure.

THE FATHER'S FATHER AND HIS WIFE

In a joint family the father's father continues to hold authority and be consulted on important occasions even after his sons have nuclear families of their own. While as he grows older and less active he acts as more of an adviser than an actual leader, good taste dictates that members of the family continue to pay him due respect.

One of the greatest ambitions of the members of the older generations is to witness the weddings of their grandchildren. The father's father and his wife act as the main hosts during a marriage and as such his name appears on the invitations sent to the kinsmen, members of the caste and friends. If the father's brothers share obligations as heads of the joint family, their names are also included.

During the formal meeting of the bride's and groom's parties at the bride's home the status of the father's father is exalted and glorified.

THE MOTHER'S BROTHER AND HIS WIFE

Irrespective of caste, a man generally feels very close to his sister and her children. The tearful meetings which follow an extended separation are a descriptive demonstration of their intense feelings for each other. This feeling is increased if the sister is younger than the brother. Therefore, the sister's husband also becomes close to the brother and both feel they can count on the other for aid in an emergency. The brother shares the responsibility of selecting a mate for his sister's children. Generally, the brother remains closer to the sister than anyone else in her natal family and is considered to be the most reliable person when assistance is needed by either her or her family. However, the intensity of the brother-sister relationship is occasionally viewed as a threat by her conjugal family. Situations have a way of cropping up in which the brother is in disagreement with his sister's joint family and the sister finds herself in the middle.

The significant contribution of a mother's brother during a marriage is not limited to his ritual participation but rather is extended to several kinds of help ranging from making initial arrangements for the wedding to bidding farewell to the guests. During the marriage of each of his sister's children, a man is expected to offer *mausala*, several sets of dresses with jewellery, dry fruits and similar items to the marrying child.

During marriage the mother's brother's wife helps decorate the house, prepare the meals and entertain the visitors. She participates in the *tel-chadhana*, *basan-lana* and *gangaji-lana* ceremonies. She is also an active participant in the singing and other merriment.

Such weddings call for the pooling of resources of several brothers and often cause a strain on their families' economy. Their willingness to help counter-balances the sagging economy of their sister's family and also attests to the fact that brothers are expected to be donors to their sister and her children. Generous and well-to-do brothers may even go as far as to finance the entire marriage of their sister's children. Also to help exult the wedding itself as well as demonstrate the family wealth, additional feasts are held by the brothers. These demonstrations of wealth, besides being prestigious, reinforce the ever weakening family ties and create opportunities for better marital alliances for their children in the future.

THE MALE AFFINES

As the married daughters continue to hold important positions in their natal families, their husbands also assume positions of importance. They are welcomed most fondly as the darling sons-in-law who protect and care for the sorely missed daughters. Their presence during marriages is openly acknowledged by the preferential treatment which they supposedly receive. In their wives' family they are respected persons, recipients of goodwill and gifts. In turn, they are well-wishers and sympathisers.

Although these kinsmen are not significant economic assets

to the family of the bride or groom they contribute substantially to the arrangements for marriage celebrations and ritual adorations. Thus one of these kinsmen usually escorts the bride or the groom during the prenuptial processions. Their attendance during all the principal rituals of the wedding is designed to place them in a significant position and to reinforce kinship solidarity. Being important figures in the set of relationships, they are the recipients of overt praise and goodwill from their affinal kinsmen.

The father's sister's husband and sister's husband usually offer a set of dresses each to the bride, the groom, and their parents during the ritual of dress-presentation. In a girl's marriage they also give her valuable gifts during the *hathleva* rite. In return they receive gifts of some value. There is hardly any significant ritual in which their presence is not acknowledged.

Like the members of the family, the positions of the fellow caste members are recognised and reinforced through their participation in the various marriage rituals. The family's social position and reputation is determined by its caste affiliation and a family ignoring the caste norms finds it difficult to sustain its social position. The disregard of norms affects mutual relations adversely and puts a family in bad standing with the caste. Since a person has to find a spouse from within the caste, a family prefers to maintain a good name. Ironically, however, the best friends and the most deadly foes are usually within the same caste.

Theoretically, the caste is an extended kin group based on blood and marriage ties. It functions more as a strong institution than as an organisation. Caste rules and norms are considered to be more important to a person than the rules governing his village. It is the duty of the *jat-panchayat* to see that marriages are made in accordance with caste norms.

Every caste bears some peculiar features besides such things as its *varna*, ranking, commensality, occupation, dietary habits and ritual attributes. As such, the characteristic features of a caste place it in a specific position in the ritual hierarchy.

In a multi-caste village like Awan, it seems to be a common feature that the castes occupying nearly an equal ritual status find greater opportunities to interact with one another. Such integration is accelerated among the smaller castes or subcastes. Marriages have been very important in bringing such groups together.

The subcaste ritual unities demonstrate how castes unite to function effectively, manage their collective affairs, and share common responsibilities under the administration of a council of representatives of the subcastes.

Reciprocal relations can be divided into two categories. The first is called *jat-buar*, which is based on the acceptance of food and water and rendering and receiving of assistance on ritual occasions. These mutual obligations of the *jat* enlist aid from persons of different castes. The second category called *beti-buar* includes marital alliances and is thus limited to the subcaste group. Even when subcastes hold a more or less equal rank in the hierarchy, their members do not marry outside the subcaste.

The councils of subcaste clusters deal with the breaches of the caste norms and enforce marriage rules such as the avoidance of prohibited *gotras*, alliances in certain geographical areas and infractions of already settled marriage contracts. Non-adherence to subcaste norms may place a family in isolation from the subcaste federation for a period of time. The subcaste councils have also tried unsuccessfully to deal with the problem of marriage between persons of greatly differing ages. Since a widow is not allowed to remarry, many a widower is forced to select a girl less than half his age as his second mate and pay an excessively high bride-price to compensate for his age. The councils have attempted such measures as setting a minimum age for brides, prohibiting large bride-prices, and forbidding marriages between older men and very young girls, but to no avail.

Among the non-twice-born castes which allow widow marriage, divorce and remarriage, the caste organisation is the chief agency which deals with disputes which arise from these situations. Their verdict is usually acceptable to all the members of the caste. For such purposes the local caste body may seek cooperation with similar bodies of adjacent villages. Small castes which do not have an effective caste organisation, such as the Rajput, refer disputes to their caste elites.

The Mahajan subcastes have a caste organisation similar to that of the Brahmin. Since each of them is numerically incapable of forming effective, independent councils, they have formed a corporate body. In the surrounding and large villages where these subcastes are numerically preponderant, each has its independent subcaste council.

The Dhakar, Kachhi, Mali, Gujar and Ahir are associated traditionally with agricultural occupations. The Dhakar, Kachhi and Mali, who constitute 45 per cent of the total population of the village, have their specific caste rules for the behaviour of the caste members. These have been institutionalised at the village level. The Gujar and the Ahir comprise only 2 per cent of Awan's population. But since these castes are stronger in the surrounding villages, Gujar and Ahir have joined inter-village caste organisations.

Even witnessing a ceremony is an essential obligation for the member of a caste. Their presence, participation, and exchange of gifts at the performance of the rituals is necessary for a complete marriage. It also recognises the newly wedded couple as caste members. Marriages are thus institutions which strengthen the bonds between fellow caste members which have a tendency of becoming weak.

Caste members are obliged to perform their role during the course of a marriage. Of the total number of 43 rituals observed by the higher castes, the women of the caste either witness or actively participate in 30 rituals. Among the non-twice-born castes, while the number of rituals observed is smaller, the participation is relatively greater. The participation of women begins with the *tilak* ceremony and continues till the bride joins her conjugal home. The women of the caste actively participate in the following rituals: *bindyak-baithana, tel-baithana, khanagar-lana, chari-jhakolana, basan-lana, binori, mandal-baithana, phere, jua-khelana, khetarpal, rodi-puja, palangachar, tuntiya* and *ratijaga*.

Of the 43 rituals observed in upper caste marriages, 17 enlist the active cooperation of the male members of the caste. The cases of *tilak* and *sagai* are put before the caste *panchas* for their perusal. The *lagan* letter is either written in their presence or opened before them. The men of the families invite the prospective bride or the bridegroom to a feast given in their honour and serve as hosts for the *barat*. The male members witness and participate in the following rituals: *binori, mandal-baithana, paharavani, nikashi, agvani-karana, ghar-dekhana, toran-marana, grah-pravesh, gathjoda-bandhana, panigrahan, homa-karana, phere, kanyadan, sakshi-karana, dakshina, goran*, and *milani*.

Each wedding is accompanied by many feasts held in honour of the bride or groom by fellow caste members. These festive gatherings provide an opportunity for caste members to get together as a group and renew their friendships.

PRE-WEDDING FEASTS

Feasts in honour of a bride are quite popular in Awan. These may be held any time between the *bindyak* ceremony and the *mandal* feast.

The number of people invited to the bride's or groom's party for the most part depends on the intensity of their relationship with the host family. The invitation customarily names one of eight different units which are invited. The units range from the bride or groom and one ritual assistant to the bride or groom, his ritual assistant, all the members of his composite family, and other guests whom he may care to bring. These invitations are expected to be returned when the best host family announces the marriage of one of its children. These feasts may be hosted either by families of the caste or outside the caste. Families outside the caste are also expected to return the invitation when the occasion arises.

The first feast organised happens to be on the initiation day— *bindyak-baithana*. The social organisation of the guests are not chosen on the basis of caste ties or status, but are rather determined by social contacts. One reason for this is that the group of caste members is so large that a family cannot possibly invite all of them. Moreover, disputes, factions, and personal dislikes also determine the extent and nature of such relations.

Living in the same locality plays an important role in bringing people together and strengthening relationships. It is not un-common for clean castes to invite neighbours from a wide spectrum of the other clean castes to these ritual feasts. Only the Rajput remain relatively isolated from the other twice-born castes of the village, and that can be attributed to their non- vegetarianism and their indulgence in alcohol. Even the Dhakar, the Mali and the Kachhi, who have practised village endogamy to a great extent and have large kin groups, invite persons from other clean castes. The Khatik and the Balai, being in the lower bracket of the ritual hierarchy, restrict their pre-wedding feasts to the members of their caste only. The minority castes and those who do not have their own strong caste organisations have depended largely upon other ritually equal castes.

WEDDING FEASTS

Mandap Feast

The main feast during the marriage of the boy is known as

mandap among the higher castes and *kunwarath* among the Dhakar, Kachhi, Mali, Teli, Kumhar, Kalal, Khatik, and the Balai. The term *kunwarath* is derived from the word *kunwara* (bachelor), because the feast precedes the wedding. The *mandap* feast is usually celebrated the day before the wedding and is the feast which is attended by the largest number of people.

Each member of the Brahmin and Mahajan subcastes is obliged to attend the *mandap* feast of any member of their caste. When a person fails to attend he is breaking a caste norm and his action will very probably result in strained relations with the person whom he has offended. Such breaches of contact are neither forgiven quickly nor forgotten easily. A conflict over such behaviour may surface years after the actual incident and a meeting of the caste council is often necessary to settle the dispute.

Since the Kachhi are among the most populous castes of the village, it is often economically impossible for a Kachhi family to invite all the members of the caste to a marriage feast. In those cases the families of the castes living closest to the host family and those with whom relations are very friendly are usually invited. The caste council has the first say in determining both the guest list and the amount to be spent for one of these feasts. By examining a family's economic position the council determines the appropriate amount to be spent. Whenever a member of another caste is invited to the feast, the host must first get the approval of the caste council. There have been cases when the Kachhi have refused a member of another caste as a guest.

The duties in regard to the arrangement of the feast are also assigned by the *patels*, members of the caste council. The council meets several days prior to the marriage event to decide the location of the feast and distribution of the managerial assignments to the members of the caste.

A peculiar feature of the Kacchi caste is that their women are barred from all sacred activities. The Kachhi offer several reasons for this unusual practice. They feel that both the process of childbirth and menstruation have a permanent polluting effect. The activities involved in raising children, such as changing diapers, also adds to their pollution. Even aside from the pollution they attribute to them, the Kachhi feel that women are naturally incapable of and unfit for performing any ritual activity.

While the Kachhi beliefs that menstruation, child bearing and child care have a polluting effect are not unusual, their barring women from all ritual activities is peculiar to them. The stigma attached to this obviously necessitates that males handle all sacred activities. During feasts women are restricted to non-sacred tasks such as grinding wheat, collecting fuel, sweeping the feast area before it has been purified, attending to children and singing devotional and marriage songs. They must stay at least 20 yards from where the food is being prepared. During the arrangements for a feast all caste members must be present. Since such a large gathering cannot be accommodated in the small house of a Kachhi, feasts are held in the Kachhi park, located in their section of Awan.

A Kachhi feast will usually include around 500 caste members. For a feast of this size, about 40 caste members are required to perform the necessary tasks. Three or four men are needed both to refine the wheat flour and maintain the oven. The tasks of providing water, cooking and serving the food require around eight men each.

Among the higher castes, feasts are organised by the families of the bride and the bridegroom at major marriage rituals. Rituals prior to the marriage are the *bindyak-baithana, tel-baithana* and *basan-lana*. The people invited belong to the kin group, the caste, and occasionally neighbours or acquaintances outside the caste. The number of guests, however, rarely exceeds 50. Since the non-twice-born castes do not hold feasts usually with those rituals, the number of persons invited is less than 20 and no guests are from outside the caste. Such feasts often become an all-day affair. The feast may begin at 1:30 a.m. and last more than seven hours. The women and children are served first, with the men eating together after they have finished. Each group sits in two long rows and the dinner is served on *pattals* (leaf-plates). All non-twice-born castes also occasionally invite the groom's party to such pre-wedding feasts when marriages are contracted within the village.

The Balai marriage feasts are usually organised by the groom's party. Generally a substantial amount is spent on these feasts, with as much as half that amount going for liquor. A Balai wedding celebration lasts past midnight and ends only when all the liquor has been consumed. Members of other castes remark

that without alcohol the Balai can have no marriage celebrations at all.

For the Balai, as with many other castes, a wedding is an opportunity for the caste leaders to meet to discuss matters of personal
disagreement between caste members, land disputes, and breaches
of caste conduct. In the hope of improving the position of their
caste, the Balai recently decided to stop serving *kaccha* food at
marriage feasts and began hiring Tamboli cooks to prepare *pakka*
food. By doing this, they emulate the higher castes and also
obtain the services of a clean caste cook. The Balai do not invite
any other caste to their marriage feasts. The Dholi and the Nai
who do not take food from the Balai may now eat at Balai weddings since the food is prepared by clean caste cooks.

Like the Balai, both the Dhobi and the Kumhar spend as much
on liquor as they do on food for a marriage feast. All the castes of
divisions VIII and IX, except the Nath, the Chhipa, the Kharwal,
the Rao, the Dholi and the Dhobi invite only fellow caste members
to their feasts.

The Goran Feast

An elaborate feast known as the *goran* is organised among the
higher castes on the second day of the wedding. The feast is
usually quite impressive and is attended by the groom's party,
the members of the kin group, the members of the caste from the
village and the *chokhala* (intervillage caste organisation), and the
vyavaharis (friends outside the caste). The size and quality of
delicacies at this feast illustrate the prestige of the family. Because
of the importance attached to this feast, economically deprived
families borrow money, if they must, from friends, relatives or
moneylenders to maintain their respectability.

THE POST-WEDDING FEASTS

Since grooms' parties are entertained for a day or two after the
solemnisation of the marriage, other feasts are organised by
caste fellows and friends. Such feasts are known as *binora*,
or *bahu-binora* when accompanied by a reception to the bridal
couple. Since these feasts are quite expensive, they are only held
by well-to-do families. Even Brahmin and Mahajan weddings
are not always accompanied by a post-wedding feast. But gene-

rally these feasts mark the superiority of the upper castes and the castes of the middle range try to emulate the patterns of higher castes.

CASTE TEMPLES

One of the most honourable and meritorious gestures a person can make is to donate a sum for the construction or renovation of a temple or the sacred places and abodes of gods. It is thought to be an infallible method of obtaining the blessings of gods, remission of one's sins and admission to *swarg* (heaven). Gaining popularity for a caste, strengthening the unity of the caste at a broader level beyond the village, and enhancing the position of the caste at the sacred level are the major goals which have led to the construction of new temples and punctilious observance of rites. During marriages bridal couples visit their caste temples to seek the blessings of gods and deities and generous donations for the temples are expected from well-to-do families on these occasions. Generally *dhwaja* (drapery), *chhatra* (a small silver umbrella) and some cash for *bhog* (sacrificial food) is offered at the time of a marriage. The money gifts range from Rs 10 to Rs 200. In Awan the caste temples are maintained with the money obtained from several sources. The wealthy are not always allowed to donate as much as they might wish, since the caste members do not want the rich to assume control of the temple and religion, a situation which might result if the temple became dependent on the gifts of a few. The villagers believe wealth is not a scale of reverence and they do not wish it to become so.

Whenever a boy comes to Awan to seek the hand of a girl, the bridal couple visit the temple at the concluding ceremonies of the wedding. The drummer leads the visiting party to the temple of Ramdeoji (the parochialised incarnation of Vishnu). The bridegroom offers Re 1 and *akha* (a kilogram of millet or maize). Offering *dhwaja* is not mandatory but is still done. A decade ago there were even people who offered *chhatra* (a pair of conical drums) and *chandani* (the wall and ceiling drapery for the inner cell of the deity), but offerings have been simplified in recent years.

A caste's social status depends primarily upon birth and is reflected in the observance of rituals and commensal rules. The interrelationships of castes and their hierarchy is revealed most clearly during marriages in which members of the castes interact with the members of the family. Marriages are also the occasions when strained relations between families are usually resolved. It is necessary that the host family must be on good terms with both caste members and members of other castes to insure proper ritual participation. The host, therefore, apologetically initiates attempts toward dissolving any differences or misunderstandings he may have with his guests. Marriages are also accompanied by a set of complex rules which at times provide opportunities for new quarrels and disputes. Efforts are made to settle any issues as quickly and peaceably as possible. Permanent breaches of relations between the families of various castes can be very harmful and are strongly discouraged. The reciprocal relationships among the families of different castes is the life-blood of the social system of an Indian village. In this Chapter, the ritual events of a marriage for which each caste renders specific services to a particular family will be discussed. The work shared by a variety of people during the course of a marriage has been classified in three categories.

(*i*) *Vyavahari* (reciprocal relationships among the castes based on mutual courtesy): Sharing of mutual obligations and maintenance of friendly relationships is the essence of *vyavahari* relationships.

(*ii*) *Jajmani* (traditional patron-client relationships): Rendering and receiving traditional services among different castes is called *jajmani*. The serving castes are placed in a lower category and are known as the *kamin* (menials). The *jajmans* (patrons) receive services from menials which are based on a traditional contract which has existed for generations. The payment for such services on occasions of ritual importance is made in cash and kind.

(*iii*) *Majuri* (contractual services): The payment for work done on ritual occasions by the occupational castes is done for a specific job, usually in cash and occasionally in kind.

VYAVAHARI RELATIONS

The Singing of Songs

The family of the bride or bridegroom begins the auspicious ceremonies with the *bindyak-baithana* rite. For this, women from the families of the neighbourhood along with those of the caste are invited to sing devotional and marriage songs. Anywhere from five to more than thirty women assemble in the host family's courtyard for the singing. Beginning around 7 p.m. and lasting past midnight, it is an enjoyable social event for the women of the neighbourhood. At least one older woman who knows all the songs must be present to act as a leader. The younger women usually know some of the songs and sing along whenever they can.

The songs are divided into four groups with five to ten songs in each group. The first group of songs glorify the gods and deities. Following them are the songs which describe and glorify the exploits of the bride or groom's ancestors. Then follow songs which honour the living members of the family. The last group of songs is concerned with only the bride or groom and are sung in the voice of the bride or groom. In the songs sung for a girl, called *ladian*, the women sing lyrics such as, "I am young and inexperienced; I am weak and fragile while you are strong like a warrior; but if you are patient I will learn quickly and become a good wife to you." The *bana*, songs for a boy, include such things as, "While I have nothing now, I am strong and healthy, my future shines brightly before me; through my hard work I will provide for you and be a gentle loving husband through all my days."

The Nai and sometimes a woman from the host family carries the invitations to the families of the women, inviting them to come and sing. The composition of the gathering varies according to the rank of the caste, the resources of the host, and the importance of the ritual activity of that particular day. At the end the hostess distributes small gifts to the visitors. Among the upper castes the relationship determines the nature and number of units of the gift. This method of distributing courtesy gifts to the women was more popular a decade ago but is often simplified to giving equal gifts to all the participants.

Friendship among the twice-born caste groups may be of the first, second, or fourth degree, with the fourth degree friendship being closest and most intense. The degree of friendship between two people is formally recognised by them and may become more or less intense only through an explicit mutual agreement. On occcasions which call for an exchange of gifts (such as biscuits, dates, or candy sugar sweets) between friends, a first degree friend will receive 20 units, second degree 40 units, and fourth degree 80 units. The rest of the castes, however, recognise only one degree in their relationship. Table 8 illustrates the distribution of gifts to members of different castes by degreed relationship during the *basan* ritual.

The singing of songs begins from the day of the *bindyak* ceremony, and the songs are sung by women of several castes, often the majority of whom are not of the host's caste. It is not unusual that the women who are invited belong mainly to castes which are ritually closer to the host's caste. The women are chosen according to the degree of their friendship with the host's family rather than their caste affiliation. The women of Brahmin and Mahajan caste groups, however, rarely participate during the marriages of castes beneath the Kayastha. The number of different castes which participate is reduced as we move downward in the hierarchy. Also, among castes with few families, those families tend to associate with the families of castes who are ranked closer to them in the hierarchy.

Patterns of Invitation

Ties between families are exhibited most clearly during marriages. A family maintains a wide range of relationships both within and outside the caste. The intensity of these relationships takes the form of institutionalised patterns when they are formally exhibited at ritual occasions.

Nota or *neota*, the local term for invitation, is derived from the Sanskrit word *nimantran*. The invitation is usually verbal.

Table 8

KOKA GIFTS OFFERED ON THE OCCASION OF THE BASAN RITUAL AT THE MARRIAGE OF A MAHAJAN GIRL

Caste	Number of families Type of gifts			Total
	I degree	II degree	III degree	
Brahmin	3	3	2	8
Rajput	1	—	—	1
Mahajan	2	2	10	14
Kayastha	—	—	1	1
Sikh	2	—	1	1
Dhakar	2	2	—	4
Mali	2	—	—	2
Darjee	—	2	—	2
Khati	1	1	—	2
Sunar	—	—	2	2
Tamboli	1	—	—	1
Patwa	1	—	—	1
Lakhara	1	—	—	1
Nai	1	—	—	1
Total	17	10	16	41

If the person lives some distance away a written invitation may be sent. In that case, the invitation is considered to be little more than an announcement until a personal call is made inviting the person. The intensity of the relationship with a certain family determines which rituals the family will be invited to, which in turn determines the number of people in the family who will be invited. Sending of invitations is again determined by the nature of the ritual occasion.

The father of the bride and the groom's family must both seek ritual assistance from families of the caste, neighbourhood and kin group. To inform these people an invitation is first sent. Following that, a call must be made to each family whose assistance is necessary. If the host who has asked for the assistance in turn does not perform his duties, when he is later called upon by the people who previously assisted him some strain or loss of friendship may occur.

The relationships within the village, among all the castes, depend upon their ritual rank in the social structure. However, the higher castes may maintain relations with the relatively lower castes through rendering and accepting services. The rank of the caste in the hierarchy facilitates some relations and prohibits others. For example the only people who attend a Bhangi wedding feast are local caste members and their kinsmen from surrounding villages.

The Balai also have a limited field of reciprocal relations during a marriage, particularly regarding the exchange of food. The Mer and Bola cooperate with them and have relations based on mutual acceptance of food but not of giving and accepting girls through marriage.

The Customary Return Gifts

The rituals which have already been described necessitate the presence and occasionally the participation of various members of the castes. When a ritual call is received, it must be responded to unless the situation is completely untenable. A person's absence from the village, the death of a member in the family, or a serious illness of some family member are the only types of circumstances which would excuse a person from serving. The individuals invited on various ritual occasions include men and women, both married and single, of all ages. There are certain rituals which require only the presence of men, others only of women, and some which require both. Each call is thus meant for a particular ritual, the family sending the person needed to fulfil the requirements of that ritual.

The women who are invited to attend the ceremonial events are given *koka*, or return gifts. Among the Brahmin, the Mahajan, Kayastha, Darjee, Khati and Sunar the quantity of gifts vary with the relations among the castes. The rest of the castes recognise only one degree of relationship. Table 8 illustrates the *koka* gifts offered to the women of the various families during the *basan* ritual of a Mahajan girl's marriage.

The Institution of Tai

A decade ago the exchange of *gur*, called *tai*, was an important institution among the Mahajan subcastes. Preceding the *basan-lana* ritual, an elderly woman of the family and the family Nai once distributed *gur* to the families of *vyavaharis*. The degree of the relationship was determined by the amount of *gur* distributed to a particular family. Relations of one degree received a ¼ kilogram of *gur*, while fourth degree relations received up to four times as much. However, recently at one of the Mahajan regional meetings it was decided that it should be abolished since it added an additional economic burden on the host family and often created ill feelings because of its unequal distribution. While some families oppose the abolition of *tai* because they feel their social status will suffer, when they attempt to distribute it they usually find that most Mahajans favouring the new policy refuse to accept it.

It should be noted that *tai* served the Mahajan families as a means of categorising their relations with the families of other Mahajans and castes. The wealthy families within a caste formed an upper class and worked out a systematic alienation of other families and castes. Abolition of *tai* was also intended to counteract fissiparous trends within the Mahajan caste.

JAJMANI RELATIONS

Accepting and rendering services, although it is based on reciprocity, has always instilled a sense of superiority in the *jajmans* (patrons) and servitude among the *kamins*. The obligatory way of mutually accepting these modes of behaviour is institutionally depicted by the term *jajmani*. This system is prevalent in one form or another in various parts of India (see Beidelman 1959; Chauhan 1967; Dube 1955a: 58-60; Gould 1958; Harper 1959; Leach 1960; Majumdar 1958 : 36-54; Mathur 1964 : 141; Mayer 1960 : 63-72; Rowe 1963; Orans 1968). Here the discussion will be focused on the role of serving castes during the series of marriage rites.

The Brahmin

To insure the success of the marriage ceremonies, the Brahmin is consulted before important ritual occasions (see Table 9) to decide the *muhurt* (the span of auspiciousness) for the performance of a particular ritual. To avoid obstacles an appropriate time of

auspiciousness must be found. The local Brahmin priest becomes
an important person from the day the search to find a suitable mate
is begun. The village priest is consulted to determine who should
go where on what day and at what time he should depart. When
even after a prolonged search no suitable mate has been located,
the priest suggests certain magical and religious rites for the person
to perform to aid him in his search. For example, the priest
advised one man to begin searching only after the man saw a
sweepress coming towards his house, advising him that the woman
would be a good *shakun* (omen). A cow, a corpse, a woman
carrying water, a sweepress with her basket of rubbish are all
believed to be favourable omens.

Table 9

ROLE OF THE BRAHMIN PRIEST IN MARRIAGE RITUALS
AMONG THE MAJOR CASTES

Caste	No. of rituals	Brahmin role
Brahmin	43	19
Rajput	40	18
Mahajan	43	19
Ahir	38	9
Dhakar	38	9
Mali	38	9
Kachhi	37	7
Khati	41	16
Luhar	40	15
Kumhar	39	10
Teli	39	12
Nai	38	12
Dhobi	38	8
Mogya	34	6
Khatik	34	11
Balai	30	6
Mer	30	6
Bola	30	6
Bhangi	28	—

A father never neglects to compare the horoscope of his son or daughter with that of the prospective partner. The Brahmin astrologer examines both horoscopes and interprets if their matching, according to the calculations of *biswa* or *gun*, an astrological unit, will make a successful marriage. Some fathers collect as many as twenty horoscopes of various eligible males before deciding on one for their daughter. Growing consciousness for upward mobility among the artisan, agricultural and lower castes have recently gained tremendous momentum. Brahmin priests claim that they will not attend *sagai* ceremonies among the low castes particularly of divisions VIII and IX but recently these castes have begun insisting on the presence of the priest at these ceremonies. So now the priest does attend the *sagai* ceremonies of these castes but sits apart from the caste members. At this ceremony he receives his traditional gift of Rs 3 and a coconut.

There are certain rites for which the Brahmin priest is asked to determine the auspicious hour of performance and there are other ceremonies at which he officiates himself. The ceremonies for which he only determines the proper hour are those which are not ritually complex and not central to the wedding. The main *sanskáras* (rites) of marriage, without which the marriage remains incomplete, are performed in the presence of the Brahmin priest. The aura of sacredness prevails while he recites *shlokas* from the sacred books and directs the participants. The central rites at which he officiates are *homa*, *panigrahan*, *kanyadan*, and *phere* or *saptapadi*.

It should be noted that the land-owning Brahmins will not entertain the castes of divisions VII, VIII, and IX even for ritual administrations. Because of this the Brahmin group has been divided into two groups. The larger group of the Brahmin population has given up the priesthood and has entered the secular occupations of land-owners, cloth merchants and grocers. The other group continues to practice its traditional occupation as priests and depends on the offerings received at the rituals of various castes of the village for its living. Ironically, the poor Brahmins are those who continue to stick to their traditional occupation which is now considered demeaning by the upper class Brahmins.

The occupational division has resulted in a hierarchy among the Brahmin and a dispute over the ranking of the two groups.

While the Brahmin who have given up the priesthood claim they should be ranked higher because they are not forced to serve the lower castes of the village, most people consider the Brahmin priests to be the higher of the two groups (cf. Karve 1965: 116).

Some Brahmin priests have begun to feel that being a priest for the lower castes is degrading. They resent having to serve the Khatik, Mer, Balai and the Bola for the low fees they receive from them. It is better to play ignorant than to impart knowledge of the scriptures to the low castes. But the village priest, with moderate means, is happy to attract a large number of clients since many more castes are demanding his services.

The Khati

The Khati, who are carpenters, are responsible for supplying the *mandap* (a rod erected beneath the marriage booth) and *toran* for marriages in the village. Occasionally he also supplies a wooden plank for general purposes. He prepares a number of models of *mandap* and *toran* during the *sava* (marriage season). The payment for these varies with the availability of the article and the client's capacity to pay. It generally costs between five and ten rupees with the cost being a little lower if the person supplies his own wood. Occasionally a lower caste client will repay the carpenter with several days of service or a portion of his harvest, but the Brahmin and Mahajan often even invite the carpenter to the *mandap* feast.

The Kumhar

The Kumhar supplies *basan* (clay pots) for the *mandap* ceremony. A procession of women from the kin group and caste, headed by the drummer or a band of musicians brings the pots from the potter's house. The ritual is observed by all the Hindu castes of the village, but the elaborateness varies with the position of the caste. While visiting the potter's house, the mother of the subject worships the potter's wheel. The potter and his wife are offered a plate of raw foodstuffs and a set of clothes. The pots are placed in the cell of the Ganesh deity with twelve other clay jars which are arranged one on top of another along the four poles of the *mandap* canopy. All the castes except the Bhangi worship the wheel of the potter.

Besides supplying the clay pots, two potters work as painters to decorate the walls, arches, and areas around the windows with different pictures. Occasionally the higher castes employ professionally better equipped artists from one of the larger towns nearby. But the village potter-painter's price is much lower for such decorations. The potter is paid in cash for all his work and is also provided with his meals while he paints at the house. When he paints the Ganesh deity on the day of the *bindyak* ceremony, he is presented a gift of Re 1, a coconut and some raw foodstuffs. The total cost is determined by the amount of work done by him. For example, while pictures of a parrot, a monkey, a god, or an automobile would cost between one and three rupees a piece, a picture of a horse or an elephant would cost between five and fifteen. The painter serves all castes except the Bhangi, who decorate their houses themselves with much less sophisticated red and green floral designs.

For some weddings the potter-painter may make as much as Rs 180, while others may bring him only Rs 5. He receives his largest fee from the Brahmin and the Mahajan, while the castes of divisions VII, VIII and IX, with the exception of the Kalal, Khatik and some families of Mer, generally keep the decoration costs as low as possible.

The Luhar

The Luhar, who makes and repairs agricultural implements, has seen his role in marriage rituals diminish in recent years. The *kankan*, a ring of iron which hangs from the wrists of the bride and groom, was once produced exclusively by the Luhar. Now, however, most *kankans* are obtained from visiting salesmen at a much lower price.

The Nai

A wedding in a patron's family is the major source of income for the Nai's family. Usually there are three types of remuneration for their services: (*i*) gifts of raw foodstuffs and money for the year round cycle of services; (*ii*) gifts for ritual assistance on festive occasions and payments for casual services such as haircuts or massages; and (*iii*) gifts rendered on ritual occasions in cash and kind, such as cooked food at births, weddings, and deaths and the ritual offerings made to gods and dieties.

The Nai and his wife each has specific tasks he or she must

perform. Others are performed by them together, often with the aid of their family. Together they construct the *pattals* (leaf plates) from leaves they have collected. Both of them deliver invitations as directed by their *jajman* to the families of various castes. They run errands and attend on the subjects during sacred rites.

It is the responsibility of the Nai's wife to decorate the house of the patron on major ritual occasions. She also decorates the doors of the house by adorning them with *bandarwal* (a band fastened with green twigs of mango and coloured cotton tufts) and consecrates the house floor with red and white floral designs called *mandana*. She arranges the articles in the plate of worship and helps in the ceremonies. When the *lagan* is received at the groom's home, she plasters the floor of the house and decorates it. Her assistance is needed when the women dress to participate in ritual activities. She also dresses the hair of the bride and decorates her palms and feet with myrtle. She helps the bride and groom during their ritual bathing and massages them with *sigasa* (a mixture of perfumed oil, turmeric, and gram flour). She also makes seating arrangements in the courtyard for the guests. In addition, she may also arrange utensils, knead the flour or help prepare *pakka* food. On the day of *khanagar* and *basan* she carries the plate of worship, digs clay for the the ceremony and joins the family in worshipping the potter's wheel.

She arranges the sets of clothes for *paharavani* in the plates, and helps in exhibiting the *mausala* gifts presented by the maternal uncle of the bride or the bridegroom. When these presents are taken around the village, the Nai couple helps in bearing the plates of articles.

When the groom arrives in the village, the Nai is the first to attend on his party. The Nai shaves all the members and makes arrangements for their bath. During the *toran* ceremony the Nai of the bride's party attends at the doors while the Nai's wife bears the plate with the material for the worship. She also decorates the floor at the threshold of the house where a bench for the bridegroom is placed. Later she attend. on the bride throughout the main wedding rites, such as *homa*, *phere*, *panigrahan* and worship of the gods and dieties.

The Nai's wife assists the mother of the bride during the *palanga-char* ceremony. She guides the bridal couple while worshipping

Kshetrapal and during the rites of the family and the village. The Nai bears the plate of worship material, a plate filled with money, coconuts, betelnuts, rice, *kum-kum*, scent, flowers and perhaps a set of head-dresses. The Nai accompanies the priest and the male kinsmen of the bride to the groom's party for the *milani* ritual.

The *palangachar* is followed by *bidai*. The Nai's wife is expected to entertain the members of the *barat* who sit on the plank waiting to accept the gifts of clothes, money and coconuts. She marks the figures of the palm with turmeric on the back and also showers red colour on their body. Among the well-to-do and higher castes she is an attendent to the bride and accompanies her to her husband's village during her first short stay there. For this the attendent receives a scarf, a blouse, and a rupee or two.

The Nai is an important member of the groom's party and attends to all sorts of jobs. A saying goes: "In a Nai's marriage no one is an attendant." He announces the arrival of the groom's party to the family of the bride. He gives the ceremonial bath to the groom and dresses him up for all ritual occasions. In a procession headed by the drummer or a band of musicians, he carries the plate of gifts for the bride to the bride's family. For this he receives one or two rupees from upper caste clients and 25 or 50 paise from the agricultural castes. He does not perform this service for the Balai, the Mer, the Bola or the Bhangi. At the time of *bidai*, the Nai receives a set of clothes, Rs 2 to Rs 5, and a coconut.

Occasionally the Nai serves the Muslims also, but not through the traditional patron-client relationship. The ritual duties performed by the Nai for the Hindu castes are performed by the Fakir for the Muslims, but the Nai shaves them and gives them a haircut.

All the Nai families of surrounding areas serve patrons of various castes both in Awan and the surrounding villages. A Nai earns a minimum of Rs 5 a year from each family of his patrons. This amount may go as high as Rs 60 if there has been a marriage in the family.[1]

The record of the gifts received and rendered at various ceremonies is maintained by the Nai. The Nai renders services

---

[1]For example, one Nai family in Awan serves 29 families of 12 castes in Awan and 15 families of 6 castes outside the village.

from the day a decision on marriage is reached. There is hardly a marriage ritual for which the Nai's assistance is not required. Throughout the course of a marriage all ritual preparations are generally made by his wife. The assistance given to the castes varies considerably according to their ritual rank, social position and effective resources.

The Lakhara

The Lakhara make and sell various types of bracelets to the women of the village. Widows wear bracelets made of glass, coconut, shell, or silver, but not of lac. Wearing coloured bracelets of lac is associated with the values of *suhag* (the sacred state of married life).

During the initial period of marriage rites, the Lakhara women approach women of well-to-do castes to supply new bangles. New bangles mark the span of purity, particularly between the days of the *bindyak* and the *basan* ceremonies.

New bracelets are worn for the length of the declared span of purity. Bracelets worn by women for marriages are usually crimson with green stripes, while the bride's bracelets are studded with glass and stones. A *chuda*, a set of ivory bracelets, is purchased by the patron of the bridegroom's family and sent along with sets of to the bride.

The Patwa

The Patwa, who do knitting and sewing, supply the *bandarwal*, a decorative band of colourful tassles for the doors during a marriage. The Patwa women also supply cotton braids and sometimes a forehead ornament. The rendering of service by the Patwa to all the castes is not consistent. The rates charged by the Patwa vary from caste to caste. He usually receives from Re 0.25 to Rs 5 and a coconut and may also be invited to the *manda* feast.

The Tamboli

The Tamboli, who grow and sell betels, are often asked by the higher caste to distribute betels, *bidi*, and cigarettes to an incoming *barat* party from their booth. Having earned a reputation as excellent cooks, the Tamboli are also hired to prepare *pakka* food for marriages. They render the service of cooking to all the castes of the village except the Bhangi. Usually the artisan and the agricultural castes obtain the services of Tamboli cooks whenever they intend to invite the members of the higher castes. The Tamboli is paid either a daily wage or an amount determined by the number of persons for whom he cooks.

Since the Tamboli do not consider their job to be polluting, they are willing to render their services to many lower castes. They do refuse the Bhangi who do not have large feasts or the ritual purity to interact with other castes.

The Rao

The Rao, who are professional genealogists, traditionally ride a horse or camel to the villages in the area visiting the families of their patrons during the marriage season.

The Mali are the only caste whose Rao lives in Awan and attends the family marriages. He recites stories of the great men of the caste's history and stories from mythology. Besides keeping genealogical records, the Rao sings bardic songs and entertains the groom's party when it arrives at the house of the bride.

The Dhakar, Mali and the Gujar at one time gave the horse on which the bridegroom rides during the *toran* ceremony to their Rao as a gift. The horse has been replaced by a cash gift called a *tyag*, which ranges from eleven to fifteen rupees.

The Dholi

The Dholi, the village drummer, attends all auspicious ceremonies which require public announcements. He renders service to all the castes of the village except the Bhangi, who use their own drum. The Dholi's work is important and extensive. Sometimes during the marriage season or during the period in which the local gods and deities are invoked, he finds himself leading processions all day long and late into the night. His drum, a wooden barrel covered with goat skin at both ends, hangs from a cord around his neck and one shoulder and is beaten on both ends with heavy sticks.

The Dholi is not allowed to enter the sacred parts of the dwellings of the Brahmin, the Rajput, the Mahajan and the Kayastha. He must stay in the corridors or at the door. He is given 50 paise and nearly a kilogram of grain on each ritual occasion. The grain is given only once a day and is occasionally replaced by cooked food. His rates are determined by the ritual occasion for which he is serving, irrespective of caste, since his performance does not change much from caste to caste, the only difference being that the upper castes hire him to serve for more ritual occasions. He usually earns around five rupees for leading a procession. Even though the Brahmin, Rajput, Mahajan, Sunar, Khati and Darjee require his services more often, the Dholi spends longer hours during the dances performed by the women of all the castes of division V, since the men and women dance separately. Since the castes of division VI have dances performed by the women, a few decades ago the men stopped dancing. Since the Dholi devote much time to dancing and drinking during a marriage, the Dholi attends them for a full night or day.

A beating drum and a dance rhythm are important for creating a happy, festive mood for a celebration. With that in mind, the castes who enjoy alcohol themselves keep the drummer well supplied throughout the course of the evening to insure he maintains the proper frame of mind. When the rhythm quickens and the Dholi is beating his drum vigorously the dancers call each other lewd names and exchange off-colour jokes and suggestive remarks. The physical contact of the dancing arouses passions so much the more. The alcohol, the wild dancing and the blue humour may be important for the occasion, but the Dholi is responsible for keeping the mood festive.

The Bhangi

The Bhangi performs the lowest menial services of any caste in the village. He sweeps dirt and cowdung from the streets and alleys of the village and is also hired by families of castes belonging to the first six divisions (see Table 1) to clean their washrooms and courtyards. For this work he receives some food every day, used clothing, and Re 0.50 a month.

For marriages he is hired to sweep the streets where the celebration is being held and clean the food off the plates after the guests have eaten. For this he receives enough food for one meal for himself and his family. When the Bhangi serves at major rituals such as the *bindyak-baithana, basan-lana, mandap, goran* or *rang-bhat*, he receives more food than he would on a regular day. He is given Re 1 to Rs 5 for the extra duties he has had to perform. In addition, he receives 2 to 5 kilograms of green corn at the annual harvest from the agricultural castes who hire him occasionally. Although the Bhangi eat beef and spoiled meat, they refuse food from the Balai, Mer, and Bola.

MAJURI RELATIONS

The general requirements of a marriage make it important for the family to obtain the services of people who can be hired for a specific task. The drummer, the band of musicians, the cooks and their assistants, the decorators or the carriers, the cart-men, and the watermen may all be included in this category. While all these tasks are performed by particular groups of people, none of the groups has any traditional obligation to serve their clients. Simple economics determine the extent to which such services will be sought. Among the Kachhi and Bhangi such services are not required from other castes. All other castes hire the Muslims to perform as musicians. Lamp-carriers are hired from Muslims, the Kachhi, the Balai, the Mali, the Mer and the Bola. The watermen are usually the clean castes, such as the Gujar, Dhakar, Mali, Kachhi, Ahir and Patwa. The castes of divisions VII, VIII, and IX rarely ask for such help from the higher castes, particularly during a marriage.

When local musicians are unavailable or a better quality of music is needed to raise the family prestige, a band is hired from a larger town. Grooms' parties which manage to bring a band of musicians to the marriage reflect the prosperity of the family. Occasionally even prostitutes who act as professional dancers are hired usually from the cities to entertain the visiting groom's party. In their absence, even professional male dancers might be hired to add to the elaborateness of the ceremony. These practices are most popular with castes of the middle range. The upper castes find this type of behaviour quite degrading and would rather spend that money to entertain their guests in a more sophisticated manner.

The Hindu marriage is a sacrament and the marital bond is irrevocable and indissoluble. The ideal of *pativrata* for a married woman as suggested by the Puranic writers implied fidelity and devotion to the husband, which was further accentuated by the glory attached to the practice of *sati* or a woman's self-immolation on her husband's funeral pyre. The ideal was so deep-rooted in the mind of the Hindu woman that *sati* was not only customary but an ideal to which a woman aspired (Kapadia 1966 : 162). Hindu scriptures consider marriage to be a religious bond rather than a contract. A marriage unites both bodies and souls, and since the soul remain intact even after death has separated the bodies, marriage is irrevocable. A couple is married not only in this life but in lives to come.

The commonest and the most popular form of marriage is the regular marriage known as *byav* or *shadi*. It is formally arranged by the parents and guardians and solemnised with prescribed sacred rites and ceremonies. Monogamy is the generally accepted pattern of marriage while polygamy is a deviation from the norm. After her marriage a girl joins a patriarchal home at her husband's residence. Polygamy is resorted to in cases where the first wife has proved to be sterile, sexually frigid, quarrelsome, or suffers from an incurable disease. In other cases a man may require another wife for sexual gratification as well as for economic assistance.

When a member of the Brahmin, Mahajan, or Rajput caste group marries, he is fulfilling three important functions—*dharma* (religious duty), *praja* (progeny), and *rati* (sexual pleasure), with the emphasis on the first two (Kane 1941 : 611). Their wives are not allowed to remarry after the death of a husband. For the Sudra caste groups, however, a marriage is considered to be for sexual gratification only.

The rate of divorce is not as high as in the West. While it is not high enough to create great societal disorganisation, it usually creates considerable personal disorganisation (Goode 1960 : 316). Considering the structural factors which serve to maintain the institutionalised patterns of family and kinship, desertions, divorces, and remarriages create a number of problems and endanger the sanctity of family life. It has been noted that young widows are rarely found among the non-twice-born castes since widowed or divorced women in their early years are remarried soon.

The mechanisms, institutional patterns and pressures which lead a married couple to dissolve their marital bond in the hope of remarrying to maintain the social balance adhering to the prescriptive ritual patterns may be worth looking into.

In Awan the two opposing tendencies have been at work in the past: (*i*) the customary practice of *sati* in which the surviving wife or wives had to immolate themselves on the funeral pyre of their husband(s), and (*ii*) the non-twice-born caste women have been leaving their husbands to seek new mates through the custom of *nata* (remarriage). However, cases of *sati* among the non-twice-born castes have also been reported.

THE MYTH OF SATI

None of the villagers could remember any occurrence of *sati* in Awan during the last 50 years. Traces of *sati* are available from archaeological findings in the village, which probably occurred between 1585 and 1600. This custom was originated by the oldest religious beliefs and was prevalent among many ancient civilisations and races. It is believed that this practice arose in Brahminical India several centuries before Christ (cf. Kane 1941: 625).

The people of Awan still view the *sati* with great respect and reverence even though the practice has been abandoned in the village. They realise that it is difficult to find a woman who is so devoted to her husband as to be willing to make this sacrifice. A Kachhi man expressed the belief that only a woman who had great self-control and unqualified devotion to her husband could sacrifice her life in that manner. He believed that a woman who became a *sati* would be transformed into a *devi* or *chandi* (a female deity).

It is also believed that a divine glow can be seen on the face of a woman who has decided to become a *sati* and that all she speaks from the time of her decision is pious, prophetic, and genuine. When her husband's death comes and she is to join him on the funeral pyre, the presence of her body will be enough to ignite the flames for the cremation. The ashes of a *sati* are believed to be useful in curing a number of diseases and even the ground over which she has walked becomes sacred.

In a more recent instance of *sati* in a distant village of the region, the wife of a Rajput decided to be burnt with him after he fell while collecting leaves from a tree and died. The members of the husband's family locked the widow in a room to prevent her, but she burnt herself in the room. While discussing the episode, a Mali from Awan condemned the attempt to prevent the woman from exercising her first and foremost right. A Brahmin man expressed admiration for the courage and devotion required of a woman who would practise *sati* but said he believed that the terrible nature of the practice is the result of the courage women possess which goes unnoticed in less extreme situations.

The memorial stones of the various *satis* come in different forms and bear different totemic expressions. Special days are set aside for the worship of the *sati* of a family or lineage group. On the anniversary of a *sati* in the family, the Brahmin and Mahajan women are served a special meal in commemoration of the *sati*. They are offered delicious dishes. The kitchen is scrubbed clean, the floor is plastered with cowdung and red clay, all the metal utensils are cleaned with clay and washed with unpolluted water, and the women are served a delicious meal. At a corner of the kitchen a symbolic form of *sati* is painted and a branch of the totem plant is also placed thereby. A plate for worship is arranged and then the food is offered. After the worship, the plate of the food, which is called *achhuta*, is served to the women. After that some food is offered to the five family deities, and to the *pitra* (spirits of the ancestors). The members of the family receive their meals only after the women have eaten. The artisan and agricultural castes offer a plate of *seedha* (uncooked food material) consisting of flour, wheat, pulse, rice, purified butter and two *paisa* to any Brahmin woman on this occasion.

THE RITUAL AND SOCIAL STATUS OF THE WIDOW

Besides being an event of deepest grief, the death of a man changes the status of his wife. The widow from a twice-born caste is not expected to marry, regardless of her age. She was once required to keep her head shaved after the death of her husband and even now some of the older women maintain this practice. Even today all widows must dress solemnly and wear no jewellery or cosmetics. She is also deprived of the ritual roles which she performed while her husband was alive. Any sexual activity is out of the question.

All women hope to die before their husbands and believe that only a virtuous, faithful wife will be rewarded in this way. A widow considers herself to be cursed and looks toward her death as a great relief. Often elderly widows go on a *yatra* or holy pilgrimage. While this view holds to some extent for women of all castes, the despair of a widow is deepest among the twice-born castes.

A young widow of a lower caste will encounter many men who are willing to marry her within a relatively short period after the death of her husband. Marriage proposals to a childless young widow are made to her natal family. Remarriage for a lower caste widow with children is not so certain. Usually if she has reached middle age and has grown-up children to support her, she will be unwilling to marry for a second time. However, if she is not being properly supported by her children or kinsmen, she would be more willing to look to remarriage to stabilise her situation.

Since remarriage is prohibited among widows of the twice-born castes, they inherit the property of their husbands and bring up their children. When the children grow up, they are married and share the property which was inherited by their mother. Disputes regarding inheritance are quite common and often lead to bitter dissension among families.

Widows of the twice-born castes observe the anniversary of the death of their husbands. Well-to-do families often invite a Brahmin to eat with them on that day in memory of the late husband. In certain cases uncooked food materials are offered in place of prepared meals. *Achhuta* (sacrificed foods) are distributed to cows, dogs, and crows. On the *shraddhakuar*, which occurs in the first fortnight of the month of *Kuar* (September-October), the higher castes hold small feasts to honour the dead. The widow makes specific promises to take a certain number of *vratas* (religious vows). These vows are believed to pacify the soul of the deceased husband and prevent the woman from becoming a widow in her next life.

In general, an elderly widow holds a high status in her family and is respected for her age. Among the non-twice-born castes, although respect is maintained, quarrels among stepmothers and children are quite frequent. These disagreements may even reach the judicial courts when caste councils and *gram-panchayat* decisions are not accepted by the disputing parties. It is very unusual for a stepmother to enjoy a normal affectionate relationship with her stepchildren. Nevertheless, a man's adult children usually establish a new household as soon as he remarries.

When a woman leaves her husband to marry another man her relationship with her children is not completely severed. The children continue to refer to her as their *asli* (real) mother and visit her occasionally.

The responsibility as the patron of a family is assumed by the eldest son upon the death of his father. Though equality prevails in rights over property and the responsibilities of a joint family are shared, yet a hierarchy based upon the precedence of birth of the brothers prevail. While the elder brother avoids direct communication with his younger brothers' wives, a younger brother may have friendly relations with an elder brother's wife. The upper caste ideals do not extend permissive relations between a man and his elder brother's wife. However, among the non-twice-born these are occasionally extended to sexual relations as well. Though such lapses are looked down upon yet levirate among the latter is an accepted practice.

PATTERNS OF REMARRIAGE AND SURROGATE MARRIAGES

Besides the regular institution of marriage, a man may also find a mate through *nata*, an institutionalised way to obtain a woman without performing sacred ceremonies and rites. *Nata* is a simplified form of marriage which takes place when one of the two partners have been deserted or divorced. This method of procuring a wife is generally prevalent among all the lower castes in northern

and central India.[1]   Children born of this union are considered to be legitimate.   Kane (1941 : 608) refers to such
kinds of women of the Vedic period who left their husbands to
join other men.   They were considered wanton women.   It
appears that the function of *nata* is to protect women from undesirable husbands.   A woman is able to leave her husband and,
through *nata*, marry legally a second time.   For this reason *nata*
has received social sanction.   All the castes which practise the
institution of *nata* also sanction the payment of bride-price in one
form or another.   After dissolving the bond of marriage, the
woman and new husband must pay a bride-price called *jhagara*
to the deserted husband.   This amount is paid in cash or kind to
compensate the first husband for the expenses incurred by his
family on his wedding.   *Jhagara* may be claimed only when a
husband has been deserted and his wife has remarried.   When
the husband dies, generally nothing is claimed by his family.
The *jat-panchayat* (caste council) or the *chokhala-panchayat*
determines the amount the second husband must pay to the first.
The sum awarded for *jhagara* includes the bride-price plus other
minor expenses.

Jhagara which takes the form of a fine includes the bride-price
and expenses.   The fine generally costs the second husband about
half the amount he would have had to pay for a full ritual marriage.   The amount serves to reimburse the first husband and
places him in a better financial position to remarry or invest
it in business.

The parents of a woman who has left her husband are entitled
to claim *mysa*, an amount of money paid by the second husband
for the woman's stay at her natal home and for the arrangements
made for her second marriage. The money is meant to compensate
the parents for the money they spent on their daughter's
first marriage.   Often a man pays both *jhagara* and *mysa* simultaneously.

Divorce is considered by the villagers to be very degrading

[1] Mayer and Mathur have reported *natra* practice synonymous to *nata*
from the central Indian villages.   It is interesting to note that Rajputs of
Ramkheri and Patlod consider *nata* as a secondary conventional device for
marriage, though in Rajasthan it is practised only among the non-twice-
born castes and considered to be low caste behaviour (see Mathur, K.S.
1964 : 123; Mayer, A C. 1960 : 209).

especially when members of the twice-born castes are involved. Pressures from the family, kin group, and caste will keep a couple together even in the most undesirable circumstances. Incompatible temperaments of the partners, a wife's domestic inefficiency, or the inability of one of the mates to bear children are not sufficient grounds for divorce. The only alternative open to an upper caste man experiencing marital difficulties is marrying a second time. This, however, often causes more problems than it solves. In the hope of avoiding such difficulties or the disgrace of divorce, the marriage vows a couple make emphasise cooperation in the couple's domestic, business, and spiritual life (Alketar 1956 : 95). A scandal which involves a twice-born caste woman is very damaging to her family, her caste, and the community in general. A woman's close friends will strongly urge her against such behaviour if they feel she may be dissolutely involved in something which could harm herself, her family, and her caste. If a woman is openly carrying on an illicit relationship she will be rejected by her kinsmen. While in extreme situations she may even be banished from the caste, no such cases have been reported in Awan.

In the hope of clarifying the various aspects of the institution of *nata*, five cases will be analysed which illustrate the specific features of *nata*.

Case 1

In June 1953, Rama, a 16 year-old-boy, who was the eldest son of a Nai family, married Sunder, a 14 year-old-girl, who lived 23 miles from Awan. Rama's father wanted very much to bring his daughter-in-law to Awan to share the household responsibilities but since the *gauna*, or consummation ceremony had not taken place, the girl could not join the family until September 1955. While working as a domestic servant in her natal village she had sexual relations with her employer. When this information drifted back to Rama's father he began pressing for a quick solemnisation of the *gauna* ceremony and Sunder joined Rama in October 1955. However, Rama, still a young boy of simple tastes who was financially dependent on his father, was unable to please the more ambitious Sunder. Sunder was also unable to bear a child for three years which further aggravated the situation. Rama's financial and sexual inadequacy led Sunder to seek outlets outside her marriage and she became involved with two young men, both from twice-born castes. The family warned Sunder against such promiscuous behaviour but she was already quite deeply involved.

In May 1958, the *gangoj* was solemnised in a village 14 miles from Awan. Rama's family and a group of nearly 2,000 assembled to celebrate a temple rejuvenation ceremony. Sunder hoped to use this opportunity to contact a suitable young man with whom she might elope. After her return she received letters from several interested persons from the towns of Kota and Bundi. This was discovered by the members of her family and her movements were watched closely. One day in June 1958, Rama and Sunder were in the forest collecting leaves to make plates for the approaching marriage season. After collecting leaves all morning Sunder suggested they rest for a while. When Rama was asleep Sunder escaped to her waiting lover who took her to his home in Kota where they were married.

The forlorn Rama returned to his home and soon found himself rejected by the villagers as an incompetent, blundering husband. When his father spoke to the fathers of other eligible girls about arranging another marriage for Rama, he was refused by all. Even his request for *jhagara* was denied because the caste council felt his questionable masculinity was responsible for his losing his wife.

Case 2

In the summer of 1960 a Mali man named Ram Chandra met a woman named Kani at a friend's home. Kani was a beautiful 25-year-old woman who had deserted five husbands since her first marriage which was consummated when she was 15. Ram was immediately taken by her charms and filled with a passionate desire for her. He asked her to be his second wife that very day. He gave her around five hundred rupees worth of jewellery, clothing and cash. When he arrived in Awan with her he found his first wife quite dissatisfied with this new arrangement. Kani suggested that she could live in Kota and that Ram could visit whenever he wished. So even today Ram Chandra is living with his first wife and their two children and he supports Kani financially while she stays in Kota.

Case 3

In 1945, Onkar, a blacksmith boy of 19 was married to a 15-year-old girl named Bhuli. Since Onkar was an independent worker, he wanted someone to assist him at his bellows. He brought his wife after the ceremony of *gauna* in October 1947 and only four months later she died of typhoid. One of his distant cousins told him about a girl of marriageable age in a village 26 miles from Awan. Onkar approached the family and decided to marry her after paying Rs 325 as bride-price. The marriage was solemnised with all rituals. After a year Motia, his second wife, died in childbirth.

The absence of a wife affected both the domestic and economic aspects of Onkar's life. Onkar attended several of his relative's marriages hoping to find a suitable match for himself. At a marriage in a village near Awan he found a woman named Kishani who agreed to desert her present husband. It was rumoured that during the previous five years of her marriage she had been living under deplorable conditions because her husband was unable to earn an adequate living. Onkar arranged to help Kishani escape one night from her husband's home and join him.

After three months the question of *jhagara* was raised and the *chokhala panchayat* imposed a fine of Rs 300 to compensate the first husband. Onkar paid the fine himself in the husband's village. Onkar established a shop to repair bicycles which added to his earnings. After only two years had passed Onkar was seized by a desire to have another woman in his house. Kishani's sister Dakhan, who had married three years ago had received consistently poor treatment by her husband since the day of their marriage. Kishani suggested that if Onkar must have one more woman, he should ask Dakhan to become his second wife. Kishani spoke to her sister who readily agreed to accept the offer. Within a month Dakhan had joined the family. The deserted husband referred the question of *jhagara* to the caste council with the insistence that an exemplary punishment should be imposed since Onkar had abducted a woman while already having one in his house. The *panchas* decreed that since Dakhan had been constantly ill-treated she was justified in leaving her husband, hence the request for compensation could not be considered.

Case 4

Eleven-year-old Kesari Lal of the Kachhi caste married Radha, a 9-year-old girl from the village of Titarvasa. The *gauna* ceremony, however, was not scheduled to take place for four years. During this interim period Kesari Lal occasionally visited his father-in-law's home. A few months before his *gauna* ceremony was scheduled to take place, while attending the marriage of his brother-in-law, he noticed another young man was taking more than a casual interest in his wife. Fearing that the two might run off together, he explained his suspicions to his father and several other relatives. They asked Radha's father to have the *gauna* ritual solemnised and to send his daughter to Kesari Lal as soon as possible. Radha's father found himself in a poor economic position and would soon have to pay for the marriages of his young sons. Needing money badly, he planned to allow another man to take Radha through *nata*, and therefore receive the *mysa* payments. Before the *gauna* of her marriage to Kesari Lal was performed, Radha was given to Kishore who paid Rs 350 in the form of *mysa*.

When the news of this incident reached Awan, Kesari Lal's father brought Radha's father before the caste *panchayat* to explain the case. The Kachhi *panchayat* met at Titarvasa to examine the case and imposed a fine of Rs 101 on Radha's father and Rs 51 on Kishore for the dishonest action. Kishore was ordered to pay a sum of Rs 300 as *jhagara* to Kesari Lal to compensate him for the cost of the bride-price.

Case 5

Bherulal, a 24-year-old Bavar man, was married to 18-year-old Kasturi from the village of Duni. The main occupation of the family is practising folk medicine. The women of the family serve as nurses. Kasturi's younger sister Parvati was married when she was 17 to a young man of Panwad village. He was a shiftless man and a poor supporter of his family. Parvati suffered from chronic stomach pains, but her husband made no effort to have her treated. Parvati was forced to go to Kasturi in Awan where she received the attention she needed and was cured. When Parvati was completely recovered Kasturi suggested she return to her husband's home, but Parvati refused. She declared she would never go back to the man and asked that she be allowed to stay as a co-wife with her sister. Bheru Lal knew

Parvati would be useful as an additional nurse and therefore agreed to keep her. When Parvati's husband asked for a *jhagara* payment, the caste council refused to grant the request since he had not performed the normal duties of a husband.

These five cases clearly illustrate the social situations and the interplay of various social forces involved in a *nata* marriage. The accounts are helpful in clarifying the five classifications of *nata*: (*i*) *raji-marji*, (*ii*) *bhaga-lana*, (*iii*) *ghor-me-dalana*, (*iv*) *ghar-me-baithana*, and (*v*) *anta-santa* or *adlu-badli*.

Raji-Marji

Most *nata* marriages take place by the mutual consent of both parties. Either the interested man or a representative of his quietly contacts a person close to the prospective bride—either a friend, relative, or a member of the caste. The details of the marriage and all final arrangements are agreed upon before the man and woman actually speak to each other about the marriage. Negotiations between the partners themselves are avoided because they often result in quarrels and disagreements among the members of the caste organisation. When an agreement cannot be reached between the representatives, often the man and woman elope together hoping to avoid the whole issue.

Bhaga-Lana

The second type of *nata* marriage occurs when a man takes a woman from either her natal or conjugal family and carries her off to his own village where he generally keeps her hidden for several weeks before disclosing her identity and announcing that she is now his wife. This action can be the result of several different types of situations. The girl may be unhappy living with oppressive parents who, because they feel she is an asset at home, refuse to allow her to marry. She may be living with a husband who misuses her. Or she may simply find herself being carried off by a man who she has refused to marry. The man may be either a bachelor, a widower, or a divorcee. Usually the two families involved are reconciled only after months of bitter feelings.

Ghar-me-Baithana

A woman may make herself the wife of a man simply by

declaring herself to be so, provided that the man agrees t o accept her. She may do this either to escape a husband who is not providing for her properly, as in the case of Parvati, or to join a man she loves or who offers security. An example of this type of marriage was reported by Iravati Karve (1965: 133). A man who owned two houses was living in his mountain home when he learned that a woman was now living in his home on the plains and proclaiming herself to be his wife. Undaunted, the man simply began sending the woman a monthly allowance. A woman who marries in this manner is called a *ghar-baithi* or *ghar-ghusi*.

Ghar-me-Dalana

A man may accept either his older brother's widow or his wife's sister as a wife. For this to be socially acceptable, the man must go before the caste *panchayat* for its sanction. If he does not, he runs the risk of being fined.

Anta-Santa

When mates are scarce exchanges are often negotiated to meet the needs of four people at once. For example, a man may receive a widow as his wife by giving in exchange his own sister to the widow's brother or cousin. In such cases both the parties need not go through all the rituals of marriage.

THE EXTENT AND ECONOMICS OF REMARRIAGE

Of the 41 Hindu castes of Awan, only 25 castes have had members involved in *nata* marriages. The three highest castes abstained from doing so due to caste prohibitions. During a course of 30 years, the 402 families of the village have had as many as 160 remarriages. People generally wish to conceal remarriages in the family, and castes which are attempting to improve their position in the social structure will try to deny that they have had any remarriage in their caste.

Of the 170 cases between 1936 and 1965, 107 males and 63 females from Awan remarried. Women have many different reasons for not remarrying after the death of their husbands even when their caste allows remarriage. Some feel they are too old or still feel too loyal to their first husband to remarry.

Men tend to remarry to fulfil the following needs: the need to gratify sexual desire; the need for economic assistance which can be gained from a marriage, or the need for a wife who can bear children. A remarriage may also result from a man's decision to add a second wife when he and his first wife are incompatible. More men than women remarry through *nata*. Of the agricultural castes, more than half the Dhakar and Khatik families have had a member remarry through *nata* while only one-third of the Kachhi and Mali families have had someone remarry through *nata*. In Awan the number of *nata* marriages during these years has remained fairly constant, at least since the early thirties. During the last 30 years only 63 women of the village have remarried through *nata*. In 26 of the 63 cases no compensation was paid either to the woman's natal or conjugal family. Often the family is unable to convince the caste *panchayat* that money should be paid for a widow and other times the family simply does not feel it is worth the effort.

When compensation is paid, it usually ranges between Rs 400 and Rs 600. It has gone as high as Rs 700 and as low as Rs 200. Generally the status of the caste has little to do with the amount of compensation which is paid or the chance of it being paid. For example, compensation has not been paid in 19 of the 33 Kachhi *nata* remarriages, 6 of the 13 Mali *nata* remarriages, and 5 of the 12 Balai *nata* remarriages.

Counting polygynous marriages as remarriages, there have been 127 *nata* remarriages among Awan men in the past 30 years, which indicates that approximately one of every four non-twice-born families has had a remarriage during that period.

The various aspects of marriage, religion and other concomitant institutions can now be summarised with the overall objective of determining what changes are taking place in Awan. The primary stress is on major changes which illustrate the general direction of social change.

Crumbling ruins of a remote past, of temples, shrines, houses and half-buried memorial stones which abound in and around Awan tell stories of other times, the prosperity and decay of civilisations, the incessant changes which have occurred since the inception of the village which are recorded in historical documents, mythology, folk tales and, more importantly, in the practices of the people.

We have seen in the preceding Chapters that while the village has its own social entity, it has never been devoid of external links and forces. Besides having historical and mythological links with the outside world, the village as an administrative unit, a nexus of kinship ties, a sub-system of political and economic activity and a theatre for religious performances, and represents the microcosm of a larger system.

Many fundamental changes have occurred in Awan during the last twenty-five years since the independence of India, which have transformed the world view of the people. Independence opened new links with the outside world. The village, which used to be a part of the feudal state of Kota, is now an entity of the large province of Rajasthan and part of an independent nation. The constrains of the feudal state which restricted frequent communication with the outside world were replaced by unusually extensive communication nexuses at an unprecedented rate. Ambitious persons who once saw a future in gaining popularity and prominence by accumulating large amounts of land and money, obtaining power by pleasing the feudal lords or gaining state administrative positions were faced with a dilemma caused by an emerging, open, decentralised and competitive system of opportunities.

The new flow of communication has enabled families whose kin ties were highly concentrated in the village to enlarge their kin circles, thus opening up fresh areas with new ideas. A visitor from outside the village is often asked about his kinship, friends, education and occupation, which in sum refers to his caste and social status. A growing interest in financially advantageous marriages has been accompanied by a consciousness of the power and values of modernisation. Education is now valued as a profound and potent tool for gaining prosperity.

The older generation which sentimentally reminisces on a glorious past perceives modern education and increased communications as threats to its authority and wisdom. Yet it readily agrees that the younger generation, in spite of its foolish ideals, will ultimately become disillusioned with its fantasies, return to traditional views, and be able to accomplish much in its lifetime.

While the literacy rate has increased tremendously during the last two decades, the most pronounced gains were among the upper castes who have a strong awareness of the fruits to be gained from education. However, since school facilities were made locally available, other castes have also made important progress. The lower castes generally send their children to primary school but rarely to secondary school. A secondary education or higher is seldom of any value to a person when he is seeking a profitable marital alliance.

Metaphysical, religious, spiritual and mystical preoccupations, with all the ritualism that accompanies them, continue to be the main foundation of family life in India. A person's sensitivity and his way of perceiving the world are entirely determined by religion; the "sacred" is pure for him and remains a structure of fundamental consciousness. Cultural expression is conceived within the single framework determined by a divine horizon and culture is rarely distinguished from the religious phenomenon. In the classical Sanskrit scriptures as well as in the local vernacular, several terms are very commonly used to designate responsibilities, norms, goals, and destiny: *kul-dharma*, the law of the lineage or clan; *jati-dharma*, the law of the caste or subcaste, and *gram-dharma*, the law of the village. Participating in a marriage makes it possible for a person to observe these laws and perform the duty of domestic piety.

CHANGES IN RITUAL ASPECTS OF MARRIAGE

Awan vividly portrays the social and cultural fragmentation of a larger system faced by a perpetuation of values and practices which are either supported by Hindu sacred books or were created by the people over their long history. The rites of Hindu marriage are reinforced by certain philosophical and religious sanctions described in the *Dharmasastras* which have served as a guide for people placed at various levels of the social hierarchy. The negation of such values and practices is thought to be irreligious and anti-cultural.

The Appendix illustrates that in marriages people continue to observe at least 21 rituals, similar in name and content, of the total 35 rituals which belong to the literate religious tradition or are derived from the Hindu scriptures which generally provide a broader outline of Hinduism (cf. Kane 1941: 531-38). Although a total of 43 marriage rituals are performed by the Brahmin and the Mahajan, who are the most conscientious section of Hindu society, only 21 rituals are embodied in the Sanskritic or classical tradition. For example, certain rituals like *madhuparka*, in which the bride's father offers a meat and wine preparation to the groom, has been replaced by an offering of sweetmeats. *Mangalsutra-bandhana*, in which originally the groom placed a necklace containing several gold beads around the neck of the bride, is now performed as a presentation of dresses and ornaments to the bride. Twenty rituals which do not belong to the Sanskritic rationale are not limited to the village itself but closely resemble rituals practised elsewhere in the region. Fourteen rituals which seem significant in the sacred books now form part of the rituals of the non-Sanskritic origin. A few of them have been replaced by other rituals, but the cultural content has remained consistent. For example, *homa-karana* absorbs three distinct rituals of the sacred texts, *Agnisthapana* and *homa*, *Lajahoma* and *Murdhabhiseka*. Similarly *devi-devata-puja* symbolises four interlaced rites—*grahyapravesaniya-homa, gaurihar puja, indrani-puja* and *agneya-sthalipaka*. Of the twenty-two presumably regional marriage rituals observed which have no evident Sanskritic rationale, only six find sanction in conveying some kind of religious meaning, while the other fourteen have neither sacred nor magical implications.

Each of these rites is given several meanings, not because they are mistaken or confused but because every ritual symbolically represents a multiplicity of meanings, functions and goals. An explanation of *binori*, for instance, may include a public announcement of marriage, a rejoicing of kinsmen and friends, a preparation for a new status, a demonstration of support by allies, servants and friends, and an unusual euphoria.

When examining the processes of transformation of the cultural content of rituals it becomes apparent that people observe both Sanskritic rituals, which belong to the great tradition of Hinduism, and non-Sanskritic rituals, which are not necessarily either parochial or local.[1] The non-Sanskritic rituals which are observed today belong to the three living generations' structures of conduct and patterns of belief. They are popular across the region which embraces several hundred villages. People identify themselves with certain peculiar practices and speak of them with a sense of pride. Caste or subcaste values are thus diffused over an extended territory through existing kinship and new marital alliances, resulting in the sharing, in some measure, of a common culture.

Tradition as well as change is gripped by the past. All novelty is a modification of what has existed previously; it recurs and reproduces itself as a novelty in a more persistent context. New additions to social and cultural life are accepted as a novelty by the people, but what motivates or elicits the desire to act or believe in a particular way is designated as tradition. Therefore all the rituals form a lifestyle. One fundamental ground for the acceptance of rituals is the awe and reverence with which people hold the past, and their respect for tradition which makes the rituals relevant even today since a complete rejection will result in chaos.

[1]Marriott (1955 : 204-211) has drawn our attention to the processes of universalisation and parochialisation. This typology has been immensely useful in explaining the diffusion and transformation of great and little traditions. Opler introduced two other terms, particularisation and generalisation to explain similar processes (1964 : 84-85). Recently Singer commented on the process of "cultural metabolism" and has emphasised the co-existence of tradition and modernity in India (1971 : 160-165).

As discussed earlier, the cultural content of the rituals is being modified, apart from the fact that the traditional mechanisms of transmission are always bound to be loose and faulty in some ways, even though those who make these changes hold that they still believe what they previously believed.

The description of the rituals (Chapters 5, 6, 7) embraces three distinct social dimensions: norm setting, status affirming, and cooperation ensuring. All the rituals thus entail prescribed, preferred, and proscribed patterns of behaviour for the people who are involved in the activity. Status affirmation is obtained through the ritual events and group cohesiveness is manifested in the value of amity between kinsmen, caste and village people. Implicit in these extensive ritual activities are the means of providing durability to the principles of caste hierarchy and ritual purity, and the strength to repel external threats and crises.

CHANGE IN MARITAL VALUES

No distinction is drawn between the basis and the nature of the marital sacrament. This apparent confusion, however, is often accompanied by a distinction drawn on the basis of caste rank. Among the twice-born castes the marital bond continues to be viewed as transcendental and irrevocable, while the lower castes, though still upholding the sacred rituals, treat the marital bond as a civil contract.

The Special Marriage Act of 1955 resulted in the codification and uniform application of reformed Hindu Law for all the Hindu population which restricted the definition of a legal marriage to monogamy. The Act also raised the age of marriage for girls to fifteen and for boys to eighteen. Another revolutionary clause in the Act permitted divorce. Generally, marriages are not registered and customary marriage practices are recognised by the Act. As a result caste councils remain very important agencies in the regulation of customary marriage laws. However, occasionally disputing parties, dissatisfied with the decisions of the caste council, take their cases to modern secular courts.

In the kin-oriented system of the Indian village, the marriage is a pageant, a demonstration of wealth, a fulfilment of a long cherished ideal. Its sacredness does not lie only in the bond but is symbolised in the rites. Though its most profound impact has been on the upper castes who prohibit divorce and widow marriage, the new legislation has secularised the sacramental meaning of Hindu marriage. Under conditions of severe population pressure and incessantly lower levels of living, child marriages continue to work against the raising of the age of marriage. Superficially it frequently appears as if a whole population is deliberately limiting its chances for better living to observe some inexplicable custom. It is commonly recognised that early marriages cause several problems, such as phenomenal population growth, poverty, illiteracy, and ill-health. A closer look at some of the aspects of the social system, however, suggests that the practice in question has several significant implications.

Indian family life is well known for its kin-orientation. Each family must satisfy the needs of its individual members, while each individual is responsible for making a contribution to the family as a whole. Despite the impression created by the virtues of early marriage, the fact is that there are several impediments to raising the age of marriage. Since an enormous expenditure is necessary in the traditional ceremonies of marriage, spacing of marriages becomes inevitable and forces the parents to arrange marriages early. The older generation feels that early marriages of their children play a cohesive role in stabilising family life and preserving the values of family unity. Since marriages are financed by the parents and for the most part a boy's employment is determined by the family's resources, the younger generation gives demure deference to parental authority. The roles of a son and his wife are now being changed by secondary and college education and by the new values which emphasise personal aggrandisements. A movement from traditional to new, secular jobs requiring education will weaken the residential unity of the family but will help raise the average marrying age. The village elite, irrespective of age, have contributed immensely to the ideal that persons should be responsible for selecting their own mates and educating themselves. Leaders perceive these attainments necessary for the village and the nation to gain prestige and a reputation for being progressive. The last two generations' preference for more education rather than an early marriage indicates a significant general change in priorities.

With the increasing resources and wealth in the family, the age at marriage of the children has gone up. The continual and circuitous change is marked by growing wealth, education and higher age at marriage. As values are changing, the ideals of family life are changing also. The younger generation is the important carrier of individualism and modern values. Legislative changes will become effective as by and large people become aware of the usefulness of such measures.

CHANGES IN CASTE VALUES

Interdependent caste relationships represent an economic, social and ritual entity of the village. Prosperous landowning *jajmans* continue to pay the serving castes in cash and kind such as grain, clothing, fodder and food. Payment for their ritual services may amount to a little of everything produced on the land, in shops, in courtyards and in the kitchen. It should also be added, as already discussed in preceding pages, that although all castes are involved in traditional intercaste relationships which include *jajmani*, the major efforts of a middle or lower caste are directed toward attaining the social rank of their immediate superiors. Emphasis is rapidly shifting from maintaining inequality to gaining equality. For instance, the Khati (carpenters) have become wealthy during the past few years due to a lack of competition, an increased clientele, and the ever increasing number of services needed for farming. Some of them now claim to be in the upper class category. Recently earned wealth has enabled them to own more land and hire more people to work on their land. They now hesitate to play *kamins* in marriages, a ritually inferior role, which to them is incompatible with their newly gained prestige.

Another example is the dilemma of the Nai, whose family absorbs the onus associated with the ritual tasks it performs during an extended course of marriage ceremonies. To boost the moral apotheoisis of his clientele, particularly higher castes, he is required to perform several menial services. The new generation of Nai, being conscious of its newly obtained literacy and the ritual contamination received through traditional *jajmani* services, now refuses to provide certain services to their *jajmans*, such as giving haircuts or looking for potential brides and grooms for a client. The older generation of Nai who disagree, respect and defend their *jajman* as well as serve them and even side with them in interfactional situations resulting from this new situation.

While the new generation does not accept the paternalistic, authoritarian, ritually superior status of the *jajmans* they are not opposed to rendering services which are mutually free from the traditional implication of superiority and defilement.

Ironically, while the Nai want to transform all ritual services from formal commensal to open secular, they also feel a loss of security and kin-like relations and uncertainties emanating from these changing values. Fearing ritual contamination, the higher castes avoid the lower castes except to hire them for unclean work. Now, however, the lower castes believe that by rendering these services they are being defiled and that *jajmani* is another form of the master-slave relationship. Interestingly, however, none of these *jajmans* or *kamins* wish to isolate themselves by refusing to give or accept services. When one group owns wealth, others need it. When one group controls a village by providing the means of production, the others must provide services to make a livelihood. However, no *jajman* is supremely powerful these days, and they do not have final political sanction over the *kamin*. Neither are all *jajmans* wealthy, well-educated and supporters of culprit *kamins* who use their *jajmans'* resources to finance bribes and buy witnesses (cf. Beidelman 1959:68; Gould 1958:428-435). Finally, it is indeed in the interests of the *jajmans* to see their *kamins* married, happy, and faithful to their masters. These service transactions will continue to weaken as long as the serving castes are capable of finding other secular means of supporting themselves.

Changes in economic activities and consequent prosperity have led to uniform interests in farming. Economic mobility is perceived to be a prerequisite for social mobility. Therefore, the developing cash economy has affected formalised social relations. As farming and artisan castes increase their economic resources, they also become aware of the uses of such resources.

The most effective use of these resources is in the political arena, since links with a wider economy have brought about an awareness of wider political issues. The growing political consciousness also brought to the surface the latent factional rivalries between the economically and ritually powerful and the numerically preponderant castes. Since unrestricted social mobility is hampered by caste values, the people are using other sources of mobility, such as numerical strength, political power and wealth. Such indices of mobility are secular in nature. Yet the most powerful change is caused by the process of Sanskritisation (Srinivas 1952, 1962, 1966).

SOME INDICATORS OF MODERNISATION

Besides its importance for personal salvation, religion has been and continues to be an important force for corporate mobility. Relatively deprived caste groups have been found emulating their patron's religious practices, and other institutions have provided them with levers for social mobilty. While urban contacts do not seem to have accelerated changes in family ideals, they have created new images of the future. Young men who move to nearby towns seeking success in the competition for education and careers now see early marriages as handicaps. In the past such efforts were thought to portend systematic economic independence and disintegration of the joint family.

Contrary to the cherished ideals of the reformers, weddings continue to inflict exorbitant expenses. National newspapers and caste journals publish special columns concerning this practice. Caste elites and political leaders discuss the problem, and legislatures have passed laws to restrict the expenditure. The upper castes consider expensive weddings and dowries to be prestigious and to assure the success of the marriage. When a low caste family is able to accumulate some wealth, it immediately attempts to improve its status by offering large dowries rather than accepting bride-price and plans elaborate wedding ceremonies (cf. Nicholas 1967:71-74). Economic and educational improvements are of no help in alleviating the problem, which has grown to disastrous proportions. In spite of moral denouncements of such practices, they continue to be the best method of climbing socially.

The agony of the high cost of dowry is felt more deeply by the younger generation who see it as a deplorable business and an impediment to progress. For example, a boy going to school or college is generally able to circumvent his parents' and kinsmen's wishes if he feels that his prospects for a happy marriage are being traded for a socially acceptable, economically profitable marriage. However, the older generation still considers large wedding expenses as prestigious. People are seeking new symbols of family prestige and new patterns to enchance status. One method which is emerging is to invite a large number of friends, allies, and servicemen during the marriage rites.

Although the local social order is conceived to be made up of ranked interdependent castes, social and cultural differences are being reduced. The deprived and lower castes now have at least potential access to the domain of greater Hinduism and sources of modern economic and political power. As low caste families manage to raise themselves economically, it seems reasonable to believe that they will spend more money on their children's education rather than solely on traditional tokens of higher status.

Changes have occurred and still are occurring as a result of secular intrusions. Thus the future direction and rate of change will ultimately depend on external secular forces. And there is no doubt that these secular forces will continue to impinge on and influence significant changes in society, religion and the family.

Appendix

Appendix

PRINCIPAL RITUALS OBSERVED DURING THE MARRIAGE

Rituals practised in Awan (1)	Rituals practised during Dharma-sastra period* (2)	Description of rituals observed in Awan (3)	Description of rituals according to Dharmasastras* (4)
1. *Lagan*		Sending a letter to the bride-groom's family, inviting them to solemnise the marriage	
2. *Bindyak-baithana*	*Nandi Sraddha and punyahavacana*	Invocation to Ganesh deity and declaring the auspicious time	Declaring the auspicious time
3. *Haladhath and snan*	*Snapan, Paridha-pana and sam-nahan*		Assisting the bride and bridegroom to bathe, put on new clothes and girding them with a string or rope *darabha*
4. *Tel-chadhana*	*Samanjana*		Anointing the bride and the bridegroom
5. *Kankandora-bandhana*	*Pratisara-bandha*		Tying an amulet around the wrist of the bride and bride-groom
6. *Khanagar-lana*		Bringing fresh clay for plaster-ing the house	

*For a comparative analysis of the marriage rituals as practised in Awan with those prescribed in the Dharmasastras, the description of rituals as narrated in the *History of Dharmasastras* has been found useful (see Kane 1941 : 526-540).

(1)	(2)	(3)	(4)
7. *Chari-jhakolana*		Bringing sacred water	
8. *Basan-lana*		Bringing new clay pots from the potter	
9. *Binori*		The pre-nuptial procession of the bride and the bridegroom	
10. *Manda-garana*	*Mandap-karana*		Erecting a canopy where the wedding ceremonies are to be performed
11. *Mandal-baithana*			
12. *Pahravani*		Ceremonial presentation of clothing to the parents of the bride and groom by kin and friends	
13. *Nikashi*		Processional departing of the groom and his party to the bride's residence	
14. *Agvani-karana*	*Simanta-pujana*		Honouring the bridegroom and his party on their arrival at the bride's village
15. *Ghar-dekhana*	*Vadhugrahagamana*		Bridegroom's going to the bride's house
16. *Badhavo-bhejana*	*Mangalsutra-bandhana*	Sending clothes and ornaments for the bride	Tying a string having gold and black beads round the neck of the bride
17. *Tel-halad snan*	*Tel-haridra-ropana*		Applying turmeric powder on the bridegroom's body from what is left over after the bride's body has been so treated

(1)	(2)	(3)	(4)
18. *Toran-marana*	*Arti*		Reception of the bridegroom at the bride's house
19. *Grah-pravesh*	*Madhuparka* *Vadhuvarnis-kramana*		The bride and bridegroom coming out into the *pandal* from the inner part of the house
	Paraspara-samiksana		Looking at each other
20. *Gath-joda ban-dhana*	*Uttariyapran-ta bandhana*		Tying turmeric pieces and betelnut on the end of the upper garments of bride and bridegroom and knotting their garments together
		•	
21. *Pani-grahana*	*Pani-grahana*		Taking hold of the bride's hand
22. *Homa-karana*	*Agnisthapana and homa*		Lighting the fire and offering *ajya* oblations
	Lajahoma		Offering of fried grain into fire by the bride
	Murdhabhiseka		Sprinkling of holy water on the head of the bride and bridegroom
23. *Phera*	*Saptapadi*		Taking seven steps together
	Agniparinayana		The bridegroom going in front takes the bride round the fire and water jar
	Asmarohana		Making the bride tread on a mill-stone
	Dhruvarundhati-darshana		Pointing out the pole star and Arundhati to the bride at night on the day of marriage

(1)	(2)	(3)	(4)
24. *Kanyadan*	*Kanyadan*		Giving away the bride
25. *Sakshi-karana*	*Preksakanuman-trana*		Addressing the spectators with reference to the newly married bride
26. *Daksina*	*Dakshinadana*		Gifts to the *Acharya*
27. *Devi-devata-puja*		Worship of gods and deities by the bridal couple	
28. *Goran*		Chief marriage feast at the bride's house	
29. *Kanwar-kaleva*		Offering breakfast to the bridegroom at the bride's house	
30. *Milani*		Meeting of the bride's kin with that of the bridegroom	
31. *Jua-khelana*		Ceremonial game played by the bridal couple	
32. *Khetarpal-puja*		Worship of the deity (protector of the village)	
33. *Rodi-puja*		Worship of the 'Rubbish'	
34. *Palangachar*	*Airinidana*	Bedstead ceremony	
35. *Rang-bhat*		A coloured rice feast	
36. *Tuntiya*		Mock marriage by the women at the house of the bridegroom	
37. *Barat-ki-bidai*		Ceremonial farewell to the *barat* party	
38. *Ghar-me-lena*		Reception of the bridal couple at the bridegroom's house	

(*1*)	(*2*)	(*3*)	(*4*)
39. *Devi-devata-puja*	*Grahyapravesaniya homa*		Worship of Siva and his consort Gauri
	Gauri-Har-puja		Worship of Indrani, the consort of god Indra
	Indrani-puja		
	Agneya, Sthalipaka		Cooked food offered to the Fire god
40. *Muha-dekhana*		Showing the face of the bride to the women and the bridegroom	
41. *Ratijaga*	*Triratravrata*		Keeping certain prohibitions for three nights after marriage
	Chaturthikarma		Rite on the fourth night after marriage (leading to cohabitation)
42. *Pavano-ki-bidai*		Ceremonial farewell to guests	
43. *Devataon-ki-bidai*	*Devakottha-pana and Mandapodva-sana*		Benediction to the deities and disassembling the *pandal*

Bibliography

ABERLE, E. KATHLEEN GOUGH, "Criteria of Caste Ranking in South India." *Man in India*, 1959, 39 : 115-125.

AGARWALA, B. R., "In a Mobile Commercial Community." Symposium : Caste and Joint Family. *Sociological Bulletin* 4, 1955, 138-146.

ALTEKAR, A. S., *Position of Women in Hindu Civilization*. Delhi, 1956, Motilal Banarsi Das.

APTE, V. M., *Social and Religious Life in the Grihya Sutras*. Bombay, 1954, Popular Book Depot.

ATAL, YOGESH, *Changing Frontiers of Caste*. Delhi, 1968, National Publishing House.

BADEN-POWELL, B. H., *The Indian Village Community*. New Haven, 1957, Hraf Press.

BAILEY, F. G., *Caste and the Economic Frontier*. London, 1955, Oxford University Press.

—— "The Joint-Family in India : A Framework for Discussion." *The Economic Weekly* 12, 1960, 345-352.

—— "Closed Social Stratification in India." *European Journal of Sociology* 4, 1963, 107-124.

BANNERJEE, BHAVANI, *Marriage and Kinship of the Gangadikar Vokkaligas of Mysore*. Poona, 1966, Deccan College Monograph Series : 27.

BARY, WM. THEODORE, STEPHEN MAY, ROYAL WEILER and ANDREW YARROW, *Sources of Indian Tradition*. Delhi, 1963, Motilal Banarsidas.

BASU, B. D., *Sacred Books of the Hindus*. Allahabad, 1916, The Panini Office.

BEALS, ALAN R., *Gopalpur*. New York, 1962, Holt, Rinehart, and Winston.

BEIDELMAN, THOMAS O., "A Comparative Analysis of the Jajmani System." Monograph of the Association for Asian Studies, No. 8 Locust Valley, New York, 1959, J. J. Augustin.

BENEDICT, R., "Ritual." Edwin R. A. Seligman and Alvin Johnson (eds.), *Encyclopedia of Social Sciences*, New York, 1948, The Macmillan Co.

BERREMAN, GERALD D., "Village Exogamy in Northernmost India." *Southwestern Journal of Anthropology* 18, 1962, 55-58.

BETEILLE, ANDRE, "A Note on the Referents of Caste." *European Journal of Sociology* 5, 1964, 130-134.

—— *Caste, Class and Power*. Berkeley and Los Angeles, 1965, University of California Press.

BHARATI, AGEHANANDA, "Pilgrimage in the Indian Tradition." *History of Religions* 3, 1963, 135-167.

BLALOCK, H. M., *Social Statistics*. New York, 1960, McGraw-Hill.

BLUNT, E. A. H., *The Caste System of Northern India*. London, 1931, Oxford University Press.

BRIFFAULT, R., *The Mothers—A Study of the Origins, Sentiments and Institutions*. (2nd imp.) London, 1952, George Allen & Unwin.

BRIGGS, G. W., *The Chamars*. London, 1920, Oxford University Press.

BROWN, W. NORMAN. "Class and Cultural Traditions in India." *Journal of American Folklore* (Traditional India : Structure and Change) 10, 1958, 35-39.

—— "The Content of Cultural Continuity in India." *The Journal of Asian Studies* 20, 1961, 427-434.

BUCK, C. H. (MAJOR), *Faiths, Fairs, and Festivals of India*. Calcutta, 1917, Thacker, Spink & Co.

CARSTAIRS, G. M., *The Twice-Born*. London, 1957, The Hogarth Press.

—— "Patterns of Religious Observance in Three Villages of Rajasthan," *Journal of Social Research* 4, 1961, 59-113.

Census of India 1911, Rajputana and Ajmer-Merwara. Delhi, Government of India. Part I, 22.

Census of India 1951, New Delhi, Government of India Publication.

Census of India 1961, New Delhi, Government of India Publication.

CHANANA, DEV RAJ, "Caste and Mobility." *The Economic Weekly* 13, 1961, 1561-1562.

CHATTERJI., S. K., and S. M. KATRE, "Languages." *The Gazetteer of India*, New Delhi, Publications Division, Government of India.

CHAUHAN, BRIJ RAJ, "An Indian Village : Some Questions." *Man in India*, 40, 1960, 116-127.

—— "A Study of a Social Institution in Indian Villages." *Rural Sociology* 26, 1961, 191-197.

—— "Chokhala—An Inter Village Organization of a Caste in Rajasthan." *Sociological Bulletin* 13, (September No. 2) 14-35.

—— "'The Nature of Caste and Sub-Caste in India." *Sociological Bulletin* 15, 1965, (March No. 1) 40-51.

—— *A Rajasthan Village*. New Delhi, 1967, Vir Publishing House.

CHAUHAN, BRIJ RAJ AND GIRI RAJ GUPTA, "The Nature of Unity of an Indian Village." *The Journal of Social Sciences* 4, 1965, 10-16.

CHEKKI, D. A., "Mate Selection, Age at Marriage, and Propinquity Among the Lingayats of India." *Journal of Marriage and the Family* 30, 1968, 707-711.

CHOPRA, P. N., *Some Aspects of Social Life During the Mughal Age*. Agra, 1963, Shivalal Agarwala & Co.

COHN, BERNARD S. and McKIM MARRIOTT, "Networks and Centres in the Integration of Indian Civilization." *Journal of Social Research* I, 1958, 1-9.

COLLVER, ANDREW, "The Family Cycle in India and the United States." *American Sociological Review* 28, 1963, 86-96.

CORMACK, MARGARET L., *The Hindu Women*. New York, 1953, Columbia University Press.

—— *She Who Rides a Peacock*. New York, 1961, Frederick A. Praeger.

CROOKE, WILLIAM, *Religion and Folklore of Northern India.* London, 1926, Oxford University Press.

DAMLE, Y. B., "Reference Group Theory with Regard to Mobility in Caste." James Silverberg (ed.), *Social Mobility in the Caste System in India.* The Hague, 1968, Mouton & Co.

DAS, GOVIND, *Hindustan and India.* London, 1908, Theosophical Publishing Society.

DAS, SHYAMAL, *Veer Vinod.* Udaipur, 1888a, Mewar Government Publication 1.

—— *Veer Vinod.* Udaipur, 1888b, Mewar Government Publication 2.

—— *Veer Vinod.* Udaipur, 1888c, Mewar Government Publication 3.

—— *Veer Vinod.* Udaipur, 1888d, Mewar Government Publication 4.

DAVIS, KINGSLEY, *Human Society.* New York, 1956, Macmillan & Co.

DERRETT, J. DUNCAN, "Law and the Predicament of the Hindu Joint Family." *The Economic Weekly* 12, 1960, 305-311.

DESAI, I. P., The Joint Family in India: An Analysis." *Sociological Bulletin* 5: 1956, 144-156.

—— *Some Aspects of Family in Mahuva.* Bombay, 1964, Asia Publishing House. 234

DESAI, KUMUD, *Indian Law of Marriage and Divorce.* Bombay, 1964, Popular Prakashan.

DHILLON, HARWANT SINGH, *Leadership and Groups in a South Indian Village.* Planning Commission Programme Evaluation Organization Publication No. 9, New Delhi, 1955, Government of India.

DUBE, S. C., *Indian Village.* London, 1955a, Routledge & Kegan Paul.

—— "A Deccan Village." M. N. Srinivas (ed.), *India's Village.* Calcutta, 1955b, West Bengal Government Publication.

—— "Ranking of Caste in Telangana Villages." *The Eastern Anthropologist* 8, 1956, 182-190.

—— "The Study of Village Communities." R. N. Saksena (ed.), *Sociology, Social Research and Social Problems in India.* Bombay, 1961, Asia Publishing House.

DUBOIS, J. A. ABBE, *Hindu Manners Customs and Ceremonies* (Tr. Henry K. Beauchamp). Oxford, 1965, The Clarendon Press.

DUMONT, LOUIS, "Hierarchy and Marriage Alliance in South Indian Kinship." Occasional Papers of the Royal Anthropological Institute, No. 12. London, 1957, Royal Anthropological Institute.

—— "Dowry in Hindu Marriage as a Social Scientist Sees It." *The Economic Weekly* 11, 1959, 519-520.

—— "Marriage in India: The Present State of the Question." *Contributions to Indian Sociology* 5, 1961, 75-95.

—— "Marriage in India: The Present State of the Question: Postscript to Part One." *Contributions to Indian Sociology* 7, 1964, 77-98.

DUMONT, LOUIS and D. POCOCK, "Kinship." *Contributions to Indian Sociology* 1, 1957, 43-64.

DURKHEIM, EMILE, *The Elementary Forms of the Religious Life* (Tr. Joseph Ward Swain). New York, 1961, Collier Books.

DUTT, NRIPENDRA KUMAR, *Origin and Growth of Caste in India.* London, 1931, Kegan Paul, Trench, Trubner.

Encyclopedia Britannica, "Ritual." Chicago, 1947, The University of Chicago Press.

EPSTEIN, T. S., "Economic Development and Peasant Marriage in South India." *Man in India* 40, 1960, 192-232.

—— *Economic Development and Social Change in South India.* Manchester, 1962, Manchester University Press.

EVANS, PRITCHARD, E. E., *The Nuer.* London, 1946, Oxford University Press.

—— *Kinship and Marriage Among the Nuer.* London, 1951, Oxford University Press.

FAZL-I-ALLAMI, ABUL, *Ain-i-Akabari* (Tr. H. S. Jerrett). Calcutta, 1960, Royal Asiatic Society of Bengal, 2.

FERM, VERGILIUS, *Encyclopedia of Religion.* New Jersey, 1959, Littlefield Adams & Co.

FIRTH, RAYMOND, *Elements of Social Organization.* London, 1951, Watts & Co.

FOX, RICHARD G., "Varna Schemes and Ideological Integration in Indian Society." *Comparative Studies in Society and History* 2, January 1969, 27-44.

FRAZER, JAMES GEORGE, *The Golden Bough.* New York, 1956, The Macmillan Co. 1.

FREED, STANLEY A., "An Objective Method for Determining the Collective Caste Hierarchy of an Indian Village." *American Anthropologist* 65, 1963, 879-891.

FUKUTAKE, TADASHI, T. OUCHI, AND CHIE NAKANE, *The Socio-economic Structure of the Indian Village.* Tokyo, 1964, Institute of Asian Economic Affairs.

GALANTER, MARC, "Changing Legal Conceptions of Caste." Milton Singer and B. S. Cohn (eds.), *Structure and Change in Indian Society.* Chicago, 1968, Aldine Publishing Co.

GHURYE, G. S., *Caste and Class in India.* Bombay, 1957, Popular Book Depot.

GIST, NOEL P., "Mate Selection and Mass Communication in India." *Public Opinion Quarterly* 17, 1953, 481-495.

GLUCKMAN, MAX, *Essays on the Ritual of Social Relations.* Manchester, 1962, Manchester University Press.

GOODE, WILLIAM J., "Pressures to Remarry : Institutionalized Patterns Affecting the Divorced." Norman W. Bell and Ezra F. Vogel (eds.), *A Modern Introduction to the Family.* London, 1960, Routledge & Kegan Paul.

GORE, M. S., "The Husband-Wife and the Mother-Son Relationships." *Sociological Bulletin* 11, 1961, 91-102.

—— "The Traditional Indian Family." M. F. Nimkoff (ed.), *Comparative Family Systems.* Boston, 1965, Houghton Mifflin.

—— *Urbanization and Family Change.* Bombay, 1958, Popular Prakashan.

GOULD, HAROLD, "The Hindu Jajmani System : A Case of Economic Particularism." *Southwestern Journal of Anthoropology* 14, 1958, 428-437.

—— "The Micro-demography of Marriages in a North Indian Area." *Southwestern Journal of Anthropology* 16, 1960, 476-491.

—— "Sanskritization and Westernization: A Dynamic View." *Economic Weekly* 13, 1961, 945-950.

—— "A Further Note on Village Exogamy in North India." *Southwestern Journal of Anthropology* 17, 1961, 297-300.

—— "The Jajmani System of North India: Its Structure, Magnitude and Meaning." *Ethnology* 3, 1964, 12-41.

GUMPERZ, JOHN J., "Religion and Social Communication in Village North India." *The Journal of Asian Studies* 32, 1964, 89-98.

GUPTA, GIRI RAJ, "Social Mechanisms and the Institution of Remarriage in a Rajasthan Village." Udaipur 1965, Udaipur University, Research Studies 3, 24-36.

—— "Multiple Reference Models and Social Mobility in Rural India." *Journal of Social Research* 14, 1971, 1-13.

—— "Religiosity, Economy and Patterns of Hindu Marriage in India." *International Journal of Sociology of the Family* 2, 1972, 43-53.

HARPER, EDWARD, B., "A Hindu Village Pantheon." *Southwestern Journal of Anthrolopology* 15, 1959, 227-234.

—— "Ritual Pollution as an Integrator of Caste and Religion." *The Journal of Asian Studies* 2, 1964, 151-197.

—— "Social Consequences of an 'Unsuccessful' Low Caste Movement." James Silverberg (ed.), *Social Mobility in the Caste System in India.* The Hague, 1969, Mouton.

HOBHOUSE, L. T., *Morals in Evolution.* (Sixth edition). New York, 1929, Henry Hott & Co.

HOCART, A. M., *Caste: A Comparative Study.* London, 1950, Methuen & Co.

HOWARD, G. E., *A History of Matrimonial Institutions.* Chicago, 1904, The University of Chicago Press. 1.

HUTTON, J. H., *Caste in India.* Fourth Edition. London, 1963, Oxford University Press.

INGALLS, DANIEL, "The Brahmin Tradition." *Journal of American Folklore* 71 (Traditional India: Structure and Change), July-September 1958, 1-9.

KANE, P. V., *The History of Dharmashastras.* Poona, 1941, Bhandarkar Oriental Research Institute 2: Part 1.

KANNAN, C. T., *Intercaste and Inter-Community Marriages in India.* Bombay, 1968, Allied Publishers.

KAPADIA, K. M., *Hindu Kinship.* Bombay, 1947, The Popular Book Depot.

—— *Marriage and Family in India.* Third Edition, London, 1966, Oxford University Press.

KARANDIKAR, S. V., *Hindu Exogamy.* Bombay, 1929, Taraporevala.

KARVE, IRAWATI, *Kinship Organization in India.* Bombay, 1965, Asia Publishing House.

KLASS, MORTON, "Marriage Rules in Bengal." *American Anthropologist* 68, 1966, 951-970.

KOLENDA, PAULINE, M., "Changing Caste Ideology in a North Indian Village." *Journal of Social Issues* 14, 1958, 51-65.

——— "Region, Caste and Family Structure: A Comparative Study of the Indian 'Joint Family'." Milton Singer and Bernard S. Cohn (eds.), *Structure and Change in Indian Society*. Chicago, 1968, Aldine Publishing Co.

KUPPUSWAMY, B., *A Study of Opinion Regarding Marriage and Divorce*. Bombay, 1957, Asia Publishing House.

LEACH, E. R., "Introduction: What Should We Mean by Caste?" E. R. Leach (ed.), *Aspects of Castes in South India, Ceylon and North West Pakistan*. Cambridge, 1960, Cambridge University Press.

LERNER, D., *The Passing of Traditional Society*. Glencoe, Illinois, 1958, The Free Press.

LEWIS, OSCAR, *Village Life in Northern India: Studies in a Dehli Village*. Urbana, 1958, University of Illinois Press.

McCORMACK, WILLIAM, "Sister's Daughter's Marriage in a Mysore Village." *Man in India* 38, 1958, 34-48.

MADAN, T N., "The Hindu Joint Family." *Man* 62, 1962, 88-89.

——— *Family and Kinship: A Study of the Pandits of Rural Kashmir*. Bombay, 1965, Asia Publishing House.

MAJUMDAR, D. N., *Caste and Communication in an Indian Village*. Bombay, 1958, Asia Publishing House.

MANDELBAUM, DAVID G., "The Family in India." *Southwestern Journal of Anthropology* 4, 1948, 123-239.

——— "Fertility of Early Years of Marriage in India." K. M. Kapadia (ed.), *Ghurye Felicitation Volume*. Bombay, 1954, The Popular Book Depot.

——— "Form, Variation and Meaning of a Ceremony." R. F. Spencer (ed.), *Method and Perspective in Anthropology*. Minneapolis, 1954, University of Minnesota Press.

——— "Social Perception and Scriptural Theory in Indian Caste." Stanley Diamond (ed.), *Culture in History*. New York, 1960, Columbia University Press.

——— "Transcendental and Pragmatic Aspects of Religion." *American Anthropologist* 68, 1966, 1174-1191.

——— *Society in India: Continuity and Change*. Berkeley, 1970, California University Press. 1.

——— *Society in India: Change and Continuity*. Berkeley, 1970, California University Press, 2.

MARETT, R. R., *The Threshold of Religion*. London, 1909, Methuen.

MARRIOTT, McKIM, "Little Communities in an Indigenous Civilization." M. Marriott (ed.), *Village India*. Chicago, 1955, University of Chicago Press.

——— "Atributional and Interactional Theories of Caste Ranking." *Man in India* 39, 1959, 92-106.

——— "Multiple Reference in Indian Caste Systems." James Silverberg (ed.), *Social Mobility in the Caste System in India*. The Hague, 1968, Mouton.

MATHUR, K. S., *Caste and Ritual in a Malwa Village*. Bombay, 1964, Asia Publishing House.

MAYER, A. C., "Some Hierarchical Aspects of Caste." *Southwestern Journal of Anthropology* 12, 1956, 117-144.

178/*Marriage, Religion and Society*

—— "The Dominant Caste in a Region of Central India." *Southwestern Journal of Anthropology* 14, 1958, 407-427.

—— *Caste and Kinship in Central India.* London, 1960, Routledge and Kegan Paul.

MEHTA, M. N. and M. N. MEHTA, *The Hind Rajasthan.* Ahmedabad, 1896, The Ahmedabad Times Press.

MERTON, R. K., *Social Theory and Social Structure.* Revised Edition. New York, 1968, The Free Press.

MORRIS, MORRIS DAVID, "Values as on Obstacle to Economic Growth in South Asia." *The Journal of Economic History* 27, 1967, 588-607.

MUKHERJEE, A. C., *Ancient Indian Fasts and Feasts.* London, 1930, Macmillan Co.

MURDOCK, G. P., *Social Structure.* New York, 1949, The Macmillan Co.

MYRDAL, GUNNAR, *Asian Drama: An Inquiry into the Poverty of Nations.* 1968, Random House (Pantheon).

NADEL, S. F., *The Theory of Social Structure.* London, 1957, Cohen & West Ltd.

NICHOLAS, RALPH W., "Ritual Hierarchy and Social Relations in Rural Bengal." *Contributions to Indian Sociology* (New Series) 1, 1967, 56-83.

O'MALLEY, L. S. S., *India's Social Heritage.* London, 1934, Oxford University Press.

OPLER, MORRIS E., "Family, Anxiety and Religion in a Community of North India." Marvin K. Opler (ed.), *Culture and Mental Health.* New York, 1959, The Macmillan Co.

OPLER, MORRIS E., "Particularization and Generalization as Process in Ritual and Culture." *The Journal of Asian Studies* 23, 1964, 83-84.

—— "The Place of Religion in a North Indian Village." *Southwestern Journal of Anthropology* 15, 1959, 219-226.

—— "Recent Changes in Family Structure in an Indian Village." *Anthropological Quarterly* 35, 1960, 93-97.

ORANS, MARTIN, "Maximizing in Jajmaniland." *American Anthropologist* 70, 1968, 875-897.

ORENSTEIN, HENRY, "The Recent History of the Extended Family in India." *Social Problems* 8, 1961, 341-350.

PARSONS, TALCOTT, *Essays in Sociological Theory.* Glencoe, Illinois, 1949, The Free Press.

PATTERSON, MAUREEN, L. P., "Intercaste Marriage in Maharashtra." *The Economic Weekly* 10, 1958, 139-142.

POCOCK, DAVID F., "Notes on Jajmani Relationships." *Contributions to Indian Sociology* 6, 1962, 78-95.

PRABHU, P. H., *Hindu Social Organization.* Bombay, 1954, Popular Book Depot.

PANDEY, R. B., *Hindu Samskaras* (Hindi translation). Banaras, 1949. Vikram Publications.

RADCLIFFE-BROWN, A. R., "Introduction." A. R. Radcliffe-Brown and Daryll Forde (eds.), *African Systems of Kinship and Marriage.* London, Oxford University Press.

—— *Structure and Function in Primitive Society.* London, 1952, Oxford University Press.

—— "Foreword." M. N. Srinivas, *Religion and Society Among the Coorgs of South India*. Bombay, 1965, Asia Publishing House.

Ross, Ailean, *The Hindu Family in its Urban Setting*. Toronto, 1961, University of Toronto Press.

Rowe, William L., "The Marriage Network and Structural Change in a North Indian Community." *Southwestern Journal of Anthropology* 16, 1960, 299-311.

—— "Changing Rural Class Structure and Jajmani System." *Human Organization* 22, 1963, 41-44.

Rudolph, Lloyd I., and Susanne H. Rudolph, *The Modernity of Tradition: Political Development in India*. Chicago, 1967, The University of Chicago Press.

Sahal, K. L. *Rajasthani Kahavaten* (Hindi). Delhi, 1958, Bhartiya Sahitya Mandir.

Sharma, Dasharatha, *Early Chauhan Dynasties*. Delhi, 1959, S. Chand & Co.

Sharma, G. N., *Mewar and the Mughal Emperors*. Agra, 1962, Shivalal Agrawal & Co.

Sharma, Mathur Lal, *Kota Rajya ka Itihas* (Hindi). Kota, 1938, The Kota Printing Press. 1.

Sharma, R. S., *Sudras in Ancient India*. Delhi, 1958, Motilal Banarasidas.

Shils, Edward, "Tradition." *Comparative Studies in Society and History* 13, 1971, 122-159.

Singer, Milton, "The Social Organization of Indian Civilization." *Diogenes* 45, 1964, 84-119.

—— "Beyond Tradition and Modernity in Madras." *Comparative Studies in Society and History* 13, 1971, 160-195.

Singh, Raghuvir, *Purva Adhunik Rajasthan 1527-1947* (Hindi). Udaipur, 1951, Rajasthan Vishwa Vidyapeeth.

Smith, Homer W., *Man and His Gods*. Boston, 1952, Little Brown & Co.

Srinivas, M. N., *Marriage and Family in Mysore*. Bombay, 1942, New Book Co.

—— *Religion and Society Among the Coorgs of South India*. London, 1952, Oxford University Press.

—— *Caste in Modern India and Other Essays*. Bombay, 1962, Asia Publishing House.

—— *Social Change in Modern India*. Berkeley, 1966, California University Press.

Stevenson, H. N. C., "Status Evaluation in the Hindu Caste System." *Journal of the Royal Authropological Institute* 84, 1954, 45-65.

Stevenson, Sinclair, *Rites of the Twice Born*. London, 1920, Oxford University Press.

Tod, James, *Annals and Antiquities of Rajasthan*. London, 1914, George Routledge & Sons. 1.

Unnithan, T. K. N., Indra Dev and Yogendra Singh, *Towards Sociology of Culture in India*. New Delhi, 1965, Prentice-Hall of India (Private) Ltd.

Van Gannep, Arnold, *The Rites of Passage* (Tr. Monika B. Vizadon & Gabriella L. Caffee). London, 1960, Routledge and Kegan Paul.

WEBER, MAX, *The Religion of India.* Hans H. Gerth and Don Martindale (Tr. and eds.). Glencoe, Illinois, 1958, The Free Press.

WESTERMARCK, EDWARD, *The History of Human Marriage.* London, 1901, Macmillan & Co. 1.

—— *The History of Human Marriage.* London, 1925, Macmillan & Co. 2.

WHITING, BEATRICE B., "Introduction." B. B. Whiting (ed.), *Six Cultures: Studies of Child Marriage.* New York, 1963, John Wiley.

WILSON, MONICA, *Rituals of Kinship among the Nyakyusa.* London, 1957, Oxford University Press.

WINICK, CHARLES, *Dictionary of Anthropology.* Peterson, New Jersey, 1961, Littlefield, Adams & Co.

WISER, W. N., *The Hindu Jajmani System.* Lucknow, 1936, Lucknow Publishing House.

YINGER, MILTON, J., *Religion, Society and the Individual.* New York, 1957, Macmillan & Co.

Glossary

ARTI	The waving of a camphor or wick light, especially in adoration of a person or one's deity
BISWA	One of the twenty units used in matching the horoscopes of prospective marital partners
BARASI	Death anniversary
BARAT	Groom's wedding party
CHABUTERA	Platform
DAHEJ	Dowry
DAN	A ritual or religious gift, usually offered to Brahmins or religious mendicants
DEVATA	A male deity or godling
DEVI	A female deity or goddess
DHARMA	A norm of righteousness and a way of life approved by Hindu scriptures
DWIJA	The castes belonging to the upper three *varnas* These "twice-born" are eligible to undergo certain rites signifying spiritual rebirth
GAONGURU	Village priest
GAUNA	Ceremony denoting consummation of marriage
GHEE	The oil precipitate of butter, especially used in cooking food
GOTRA	An exogamous clan usually originating from historical or mythical antecedents
GUR or GUD	Unrefined brown sugar made from sugarcane juice
JAGIRDAR	A feudal chief
JAJMAN	A term used for patrons for all service-rendering castes
JATI	Refers to an endogamous group manifesting certain ritual and functional attributes indicative of its probable rank in the social hierarchy
JWARA	Millet sprouts
KACCHA	Literally, raw; unripe, especially unfried foods cooked with water and salt. Such foods entail several prohibitions within and across the castes and subcastes. The word is also used in reference to mud walls and roads
KAMIN	Menial servant. Collectively refers to castes who generally render menial services

KANYADAN	One of the essential rites in Hindu marriage connoting "offering of a virgin"
KATHA-VACHAK	A person, usually a priest, who recites sacred stories
KRIYA-KARMA	Propitiatory rites for salvation of the soul of the dead
KSHETRAPAL	A deity presiding over a region
LAGAN	Formal reminder of the wedding day
LINGAM	Literally, phallus, one of the most common symbols of Siva
GRAHASTHASHRAM	The householder's life; one of the four stages in the life of a Hindu
MANTRA	A spell; generally refers to a ritual incantation
MOHALLA	A residential locality
MUHURT	The span of auspiciousness
NATA	Remarriage; especially by a couple in which either partner was first wedded through full rites of marriage
NEG	Payment in cash or kind for a ritual service
NIMANTRAN or NYOTA	Verbal or written invitation
PANCHA	Member of a council
PAKKA	Kinds of food usually fried in butter or oil; generally used in intercaste feasts. The word also refers to houses and roads made of solid stone and concrete
PATIVRATA	A virtuous woman; a norm expressing a woman's complete devotion to her husband
RUPEE	The denomination of currency in India; a rupee is equal to a hundred paisa. An American dollar is approximately equal to Rs 7.50
SAMSKAR	Rites performed according to the scriptures by every Hindu
SAROPAV	Gift of clothes, cash, and a coconut especially offered in certain marriage rituals
SATI	Wife's self immolation on her husband's funeral pyre as a mark of devotion; also, memorial tombs of such women
SEEDHA	Usually a plate of raw and uncooked foods offered to a Brahmin
SHLOKAS	Hymns from the Hindu scriptures
TILAK	Crimson or sandalpaste mark(s) on the forehead; also a ritual declaring a boy a prospective groom
VARANA	A rite according a reception to a person, usually to complete a ceremony
VARNA	A category in the four level classification of Hindu society. The upper three are known as the "twice-born". An ideal scheme representing certain principles as a basis of the caste system
VIVAH	Wedding, marriage